Small-Unit Leaders' Guide

to

Counterinsurgency

June 2006

Published by Books Express Publishing
Copyright © Books Express, 2010
ISBN 978-1-907521-29-1
To purchase copies at discounted prices please contact
info@books-express.com

UNITED STATES MARINE CORPS
Commanding General, Marine Corps Combat Development Command
Deputy Commandant for Combat Development and Integration

20 June 2006

FOREWORD

We are a Nation at war and will remain so for the foreseeable future. To better prepare our Marines for that war, this volume provides a collection of counterinsurgency tactics, techniques and procedures (TTP). These TTP represent the current "best practices" derived from American, Australian and British sources. Written *by* small unit leaders *for* small unit leaders, they have been specifically crafted for application at the company level and below. The reader will find variations on style and format between the various chapters and annexes. That is intentional, as the operational demand places greater priority on timeliness of delivery rather than the niceties of presentation.

While these TTP provide proven methods for the day-to-day practice of counterinsurgency, they are not intended to be prescriptive. By necessity, our small unit leaders will adapt the ideas presented herein to meet the needs of their own unique circumstances. As the war progresses, we can also expect the enemy to adapt his TTP—further necessitating continued innovation and adaptation on our part. The "shelf life" of this edition will therefore be relatively short, as continued feedback from the operating forces will provide the means of refining and updating the content of subsequent editions.

J. N. MATTIS
Lieutenant General, U.S. Marine Corps

Tactics, Techniques, and Procedures for Counterinsurgency

CONTENTS

iv

CHAPTER 1

Overview

Marine Corps Operating Concepts for a Changing Security Environment describes Marine Corps forces that will be organized, based, trained and equipped for forward presence, security cooperation, counterterrorism, crisis response, forcible entry, prolonged operations and counterinsurgency. The Tentative Manual for Countering Irregular Threats: an Updated Approach to Counterinsurgency Operations, and Countering Irregular Threat—A Comprehensive Approach, elaborate on counterinsurgency operations at higher echelons of command. However, counterinsurgency is warfare characterized by small unit action. This handbook provides a guide for the small unit leader.

Purpose

This handbook provides the tactics, techniques, and procedures that may be applied by small unit leaders engaged in counterinsurgency. It is principally focused at the company and below. It describes the nature of insurgency and counterinsurgency, common insurgent approaches, preparation for counterinsurgency, mobilizing the populace, information and intelligence operations, and operations in a counterinsurgency environment. The handbook is not prescriptive but meant to inform. The specific aspects of each conflict combined with small unit leader judgment and initiative will drive how to apply the ideas within the handbook.

Understanding Insurgency

Insurgencies date to the earliest forms of government and will continue to exist as long as the governed harbor grievances against authority that they believe cannot be resolved by peaceful means.

What is an insurgency? The Department of Defense (DOD) defines insurgency as "an organized movement aimed at the overthrow of a constituted government through use of subversion and armed conflict." Simply put, an insurgency is a struggle between a non-ruling group and their ruling authority. Insurgents use political resources, to include the increased use of the media and international opinion, as well as violence to destroy the political legitimacy of the ruling authority and build their

1

own political legitimacy and power.[1] Examples of this type of warfare range from the American Revolution to the present situation in Iraq. The conflict itself can range from acts of terrorism to the more conventional use of the media to sway public opinion. Whatever form the insurgency takes, it serves an ideology or political goal.

What are the root causes of an insurgency? For an insurgency to flourish, a majority of the population must either support or remain indifferent to insurgent ideals and practices. There must be a powerful reason that drives a portion of the populace to armed opposition against the existing government. Grievances may have a number of causes, such the lack of economic opportunity, restrictions on basic liberties, government corruption, ethnic or religious tensions, or the presence of an occupying force. It is through this line of thought or ideal that insurgents attempt to mobilize the population.

Understanding Counterinsurgency

What is counterinsurgency?—DOD defines counterinsurgency as "those military, paramilitary, political, economic, psychological, and civic actions taken by a government to defeat insurgency. Also called "COIN." The United States uses a wide breadth of national capabilities to defeat insurgencies through a variety of means. The Department of State (DOS), Central Intelligence Agency (CIA) and Department of Justice (DOJ) use country teams to generate strategic objectives and assist the host nation government. The military may support those efforts by employing conventional forces, in combination with Special Operations Forces (SOF), in a variety of activities aimed at enhancing security and/or alleviating causes of unrest.

What is the likely role of the military? While military forces may be the most visible sign of U.S. involvement, especially in the early phases of a counterinsurgency, they play a supporting role to the political and economic initiatives designed to enhance the effectiveness legitimacy of the government. Establishing a secure environment for these initiatives is normally a primary objective of military forces and can take many forms. This can be a minimal requirement to support host nation forces

---

[1] United States Marine Corps 2006, *Tentative Manual for Countering Irregular Threats: A New Approach to Counterinsurgency Operations* (Pg 5). Referenced from **Bard E O'Neill**, *Insurgency and Terrorism*, (Dulles, VA: Brassey's Inc, 1990, (Pg 13))

with advisors and equipment or it can mean a large scale- commitment of U.S. forces to carryout the preponderance of operations. In addition to providing a secure environment, U.S. military forces may also be called upon to support infrastructure development, provide health services, conduct police functions, or directly target insurgent cells. Given the wide range of potential military contributions, it is imperative that all military personnel understand how their actions and decisions must support the overall campaign design to de-legitimize the insurgency in the eyes of the population. Significantly, successful counterinsurgencies are normally measured in years or even decades and require a unity of effort across the spectrum of U.S. agencies.

How can I learn to counter a specific insurgency? Chapter 5 of this volume provides detailed information that can assist unit leaders in developing an understanding of a specific insurgency in order to develop effective counter measures. Additionally, the United Kingdom has produced an excellent *Land Component Handbook,* from which the list below was extracted.[2] It provides a broad approach that may have utility conducting mission analysis.

- *The insurgency force, the civil population and the terrain are virtually inseparable factors in guerrilla warfare.*

- *What is the structural organization of the insurgent group?* Identification? Composition? Overall organizational characteristics: strength; combat efficiency; status of training; means of communications; morale and discipline? Ideology?

- *Where are the insurgent groups located?* Guerrilla camps? Assembly points? Rendezvous points? Trails?

- *What is the insurgent group's method of operations?* Political? Economic? Converting? Propaganda? Types of tactics employed? Insurgent aims?

- *How is the insurgent group armed and equipped?* Supply source of food and commodities? Weapons and ammunition? Means of providing logistic support?

---

[2] Section 22—Counterinsurgency Operations, Land Component Handbook, Issue 1.0 dated Aug 01.

- *What are the factors which cause or contribute to the development and continuation that motivate the insurgent group?*

- *What is the relationship between the insurgent group and the population?*

- *What is the relationship with any external forces?*

- *What are the psychological vulnerabilities of the insurgent group?*

- *What is the identification of any hostile, uncommitted or friendly elements that may be assisting the insurgent group?* Location? Name? Organizational structure?

- *What are the insurgent group's motivations and loyalties to the various elements of the population*

- *What is the size and proportion of the civil population that is likely to actively support the insurgent group?*

- *What are the effects of the local authorities and police on the civil population?*

- *What are the capabilities of the local populace to provide food, supplies, shelter, etc. to the insurgent group?* Type? Amount? Method? Location?

- *What are the capabilities of the local populace to provide food, supplies, shelter, etc. to friendly forces?* Type? Amount? Method? Location?

- *What is the availability of water and fuel?*

- *What are the vulnerabilities of the friendly civil populace?*

CHAPTER 2

Common Insurgent Approaches

This chapter describes common insurgent approaches toward achieving their goals. Most insurgencies are fighting a war of ideas and attempt to mobilize a population towards a single line of thought or ideology. For example, in the American Revolution the single thought was one of independence from "British Tyranny." The ideas behind the *Declaration of Independence* united the Colonies against British rule. The ideology behind each insurgency will be unique. This chapter presents some recurring themes and tactics that will help you understand the nature of your specific fight.

Networked Operations

A key to understanding insurgencies is recognition that insurgents use a distributed network, motivated by the common ideology, to mobilize the population to their cause. Insurgent networks are often a trusted group of individuals created through family/ marriage, tribal, business, religious, political and/or social relationships. Family and tribal ties create a strong core that insurgent groups leverage to link to various political, social and business arms of the populace. A single family may only have a small number of active insurgents; however, marriage, friendship and group ties can extend communications, support and loyalty. A local-national who might otherwise turn in an insurgent will not divulge information that may eventually harm a family member.

Networks provide the insurgency a means to rapidly spread information and intelligence, and enable the logistics support and communication necessary for distributed operations. Insurgents leverage relationships and networking to tie to trans-national terrorist groups, political wings, academic institutions, local business, and social groups. *Understanding these relationships and networks is essential in undermining the insurgents' efforts to mobilize support.*

Persuasion, Coercion and Intimidation

Insurgents use a combination of persuasion, coercion and intimidation to influence a population. Perception and use of information are critical to insurgent success. Insurgents base their actions on their capabilities and intentions. Insurgents can employ a huge variety of tactics. Typical insurgent tactics and operations include, but are not limited to:

Ambushes—Used to create maximum damage and create an illusion of insurgent strength among the local civilian populace. They can also be used to capture and publicly torture individuals to further terrorize local civilians, counterinsurgency forces and the international community.

- *Vehicle Ambushes*—Often initiated via improvised explosive devises (IED), vehicle-borne IED or rocket propelled grenades (RPG) to stop a convoy or vehicle patrol and establish a kill zone. Normally these are used for disruptions, slowing logistics and *bogging down* the counterinsurgency force. In some instances insurgents will use convoy or vehicle ambushes to acquire supplies and munitions. Vehicle ambushes are most effective in tight city streets where insurgents can establish well defined kill zones and secondary anti-personnel devices used against dismounting troops. The close quarters eliminate the vehicle's maneuverability and the complexity of the terrain makes it difficult to fire from a turret.

- *Personnel Ambushes*—Personnel ambushes can be used to deny a patrol access to an area as a defensive action as well as for the destruction or capture of individuals. Like any patrol, they are planned in detail and are seldom random.

Assassination—A term generally applied to the killing of prominent persons and symbolic personnel as well as "traitors" who defect from the group, human intelligence (HUMINT) sources, and others who work with/for the government or U.S. forces.

Arson—Less dramatic than most tactics, arson has the advantage of low risk to the perpetrator and requires only a low level of technical knowledge.

Bombing and High Explosives—The IED is currently the insurgent's weapon of choice, followed by suicide bombing. They gain publicity for the insurgent cause while providing the ability to control casualties through selective placement of the device timed detonation. They also allow the insurgents to deny responsibility should the action produce undesirable results. Critical to our mission is the ability to deny the time and place for detonation. For more information on IEDs, see Annex D.

Civil Operations—In many cases insurgent organizations or the political wing that supports them will conduct civil type operations (e.g. give money to schools and poor families, aide in religious or child development activities) to virtually replace the government in communities that support them. The purpose of these operations is to create legitimacy, presenting the insurgency as a responsible and moral organization.

Deliberate Attacks—In recent conflicts deliberate, coordinated attacks served as mostly psychological and informational operations. Their goal is to create as much destruction as possible without owning any terrain. Generating shock, fear and publicity is generally the main purpose of these attacks. This does not mean the attacks are ineffective militarily; the strategic effect generated can cause policy change, shifts in international opinion and can destroy local trust in coalition security.

Demonstrations—Can be used to incite violent responses by counterinsurgents and also to display the popularity of the insurgency cause.

Denial and Deception—Denial involves measures taken by the threat to block, prevent, or impair U.S. intelligence collection. Examples include killing or otherwise intimidating HUMINT sources. Deception involves manipulating information and perceptions in order to mislead.

Hijacking or Skyjacking—Sometimes employed as a means of escape, hijacking is normally carried out to produce a spectacular hostage situation. Although trains, buses, and ships have been hijacked, aircraft are the preferred target because of their greater mobility and because they are difficult to penetrate during terrorist operations.

Hoaxes—Any insurgent or terrorist group that has established credibility can employ a hoax with considerable success. A threat against a person's life causes that person and those associated with that individual to devote time and efforts to security measures. A bomb threat can close a commercial building, empty a theater, or delay an aircraft flight at no cost to the insurgent or terrorist. False alarms desensitize and dull the efficiency of security personnel, thus degrading readiness while undermining the moral authority of the local government and creating doubt within the population.

Hostage Taking—This is an overt seizure of one or more individuals with the intent of gaining publicity or other concessions in return for release of the hostage. While dramatic, hostage and hostage barricade situations are risky for the perpetrator

Indirect Fire—Insurgents may use indirect fire to harass counterinsurgents, or to cause them to commit forces that are attacked by secondary ambushes.

Infiltration and Subversion—Gain intelligence and degrade the effectiveness of government organizations by getting them to hire insurgent agents or by convincing members of the government to support the insurgency. Subversion may be achieved through intimidation, indoctrination of sympathetic individuals, or bribes.

Information—The aggressive use of information to influence and promote insurgent ideals and discredit a government or counterinsurgency. Insurgents leverage networks and information technologies to penetrate the local population and broadcast their message regionally and globally. Using information much like an advertising or marketing company every effort is made to "sell" their value and ideas while driving a wedge between the population and those opposing the insurgency. At times the insurgent will lie, sensationalize, and exaggerate or modify the truth leaving the counterinsurgent to explain the truth. The largest information outlet insurgents have to the international community is the news media. Many operations are used to generate attention from international news groups such as CNN and BBC. Insurgents will allow reporters access to their operations in an attempt to either gain international sympathy or create terror amongst the citizens of coalition nations.

Kidnapping—While similar to hostage taking, kidnapping has significant differences. Kidnapping is usually a covert seizure of one or more specific persons in order to extract specific demands. It is normally the most difficult task to execute. The perpetrators of the action may or may not be known for a long time. Media attention is initially intense, but decreases over time. Because of the time involved, successful kidnapping requires elaborate planning and logistics. The risk to the perpetrators may be less than in the hostage situation.

Propaganda—Insurgents may disseminate propaganda using any form of media, as well as face-to-face talks.

Raids or Attacks on Facilities—Armed attacks on facilities are usually undertaken to:

- Demonstrate the government's inability to secure critical facilities or national symbols.

- Acquire resources (for example, robbery of a bank or armory).

- Kill U.S. and or government personnel.

- Intimidate the government and the populace.

Sabotage—The objective in most sabotage incidents is to demonstrate how vulnerable a particular society, or government, is to terrorist actions. Industrialized areas provide especially vulnerable targets. Utilities, communications, and transportation systems are so interdependent that a serious disruption of any one affects all of them and gains immediate public attention. Sabotage of industrial or commercial facilities is one means of creating significant disruption while making a statement of future intent. Military facilities and installations, information systems, and information infrastructures may become targets of terrorist sabotage.

Seizure—Seizure usually involves a building or object that has value in the eyes of the audience. There is some risk to the perpetrator because security forces have time to react.

Terror and crime—Although most forms of insurgent actions are used to generate some form of terror, tactics such as ambushes and attacks can be justified as interactions between two armed forces. There are other actions however, that are clearly terrorist or criminal in nature. Some examples are: Deliberately targeting civilians or civilian leadership; Beheadings, hangings, burnings and other forms of public torture; Kidnappings (either to torture or for monetary gain); Drug smuggling or selling; Theft & other organized crime

Weapons of Mass Destruction/Effects—Some insurgent groups may possess chemical and biological (CB) weapons, and there is a potential for use of CB weapons in the future. These weapons, relatively cheap and easy to make, may be used in place of conventional explosives in many situations. The potential for mass destruction and the deep-seated fear most people have for CB weapons could be attractive to a group wishing to attract international attention. Although an explosive nuclear device is acknowledged to be beyond the financial and/or technical reach of most terrorist groups, a CB weapon or even a radiological dispersion device using nuclear contaminants is not. The technology is simple and the payoff is potentially higher than conventional explosives.

CHAPTER 3

Preparation for Counterinsurgency

The time prior to deployment is critical and must be used wisely. Pre-deployment training and preparation is most likely the last time you will be able to analyze the situation without the pressures of a fluid and violent environment constantly surrounding you. Maximize this time; make use of every means to understand your operating area, the problems, and people in it. Take note of the following checklists and delegate the tasks to ensure that workload, knowledge and understanding are disseminated throughout your unit. Mission type orders are essential in the prosecution of COIN operations in that they are based on mutual trust in the chain of command. Give subordinate leaders responsibility and trust, and then evaluate them in detail. Once you are in the situation, success will only be achieved if you trust their ability to seize every opportunity to legally, ethically, and morally carry out their duties and accomplish the mission.

Intelligence Preparation

> *Know your patch. Know the people, the topography, economy, history and culture. Know every village, road, field, population group, tribal leader and ancient grievance. Your task is to become the world expert on your particular district... Neglect this knowledge, and it will kill you.*
> —*Dr David Kilcullen, 2006*

To be effective in a counterinsurgency operation you must understand more than the enemy's composition, disposition and strength. A quick *METT-T* analysis is not enough to create the depth of understanding needed to positively affect an area. You have to understand the area as a whole. To be effective you must first become an expert in your area of responsibility and know how it ties into and relates to the areas surrounding it. This knowledge will become the basis for your planning and execution, and how to adapt to the inevitable changes as operations progress in your area.

Make contact and maintain open communication with the current commander on the ground via phone, email or personal liaison. Ask for any turnover information he may have and any additional lessons learned he acquired while there. Prepare specific questions to fill your gaps and holes; remember, although the commander will most likely be more than willing to aid his replacement, he is still in the fight. Do not waste his time by making him guess what information you need.

Intelligence Preparation of the Operations Area (IPOA) Checklist: Our current intelligence gathering process has been optimized for conventional warfare and cannot reveal the level of detail required for COIN operations. To be effective it is critical that locally applicable information and intelligence on the local cultural, informational and operational terrain is gathered, understood and applied to operational planning and activity. The following checklist represents an outline IPOA.

- ***Culture***

    - ***Language(s)***? Major dialects? Language taught in school? Availability of interpreters?

    - ***Religion(s)?*** Types? Beliefs? Traditions? Holy days / places / books? Clergy / leaders and their place in the community?

    - ***Tribes?*** How / how long / why are they allied with or opposed to other each other? Customs? Religious ties? Political affiliations? Means of commerce?

    - ***Traditional roles of men and women?***

    - ***Local customs / traditions / holidays?***

    - ***Families?*** Influential families? Connections to other families? Family leaders? Role of the family in the community / tribe?

- ***Economy***

    - ***Means of income and distribution?*** Key industries and markets? Central market areas? Popular shops and cafes? Forms of commerce and trade? Key industrial leaders and merchants?

    - ***Standard of living?*** Divisions between wealthy, middle, and low income? Effect of current hostilities on the economy?

12

- *Civil Infrastructure.* Water? Food? Sewer? Health care? Electric? Fire department? Police department?

- *Terrain*

  - *Key terrain?* Buildings and infrastructure? Lines of communication: roads and railways; waterways; trails; tunnels and brides?

  - *Insurgent occupied / dominated areas?*
  - *Obstacles?*

  - *Religious and cultural areas?* Where are they and what do they mean?

- *Military / Para-military*

  - *Host nation military in the area?* Units? Composition, disposition and strength? Effectiveness? (Morale, training, experience, advisors, liaisons, means of communication?)

  - *Government sponsored militia in the area?*

  - *Non-government sponsored militia in the area?*

- *Enemy*

  - *Popular mobilization?* Single narrative? Civil projects? Connection to the populace? Connection to the narrative?

  - *Key leaders?* Decision makers? Operations leaders? Connecting files? Daily routine?

  - *Networking?* Family relationships: immediate and extended? Friendships? Tribal relationships? Business relationships? Income, interests, industry and alignments? (Internal and external sources of income; connections to other industries; interests in political offices and other power bases; alignments with nongovernmental organizations, transnational extremists

13

organizations, academic organizations, religious groups or
political parties?)

- *Activity?* Recent actions such as assaults, raids, ambushes, etc.?
  (Locations; times; specific actions; goals; success?) Recent
  arrests? Counter actions? Recent civil / humanitarian actions?

- *Composition, disposition, and strength?* Weapons? Tribal garb?
  Size of operational elements? General strength of the force?
  Most probable course of action?

- **Other Elements**

  - *Nongovernmental organizations in the area?*

  - *Other government agencies in the area?*

  - *Special operations forces in the area?*

Build Diagrams and Charts—As you build your situational awareness
of the environment you must create easy to understand, adaptable and
accurate diagrams and information sheets which complement one another
and allow you and your unit to acquire knowledge and contribute to the
understanding of the situation. The information must be displayed so that
all members of your unit are kept informed and can act on the
information. Diagrams and charts lead to an understanding of the
insurgents means of operations; these same diagrams are useful for
understanding tribal, family, non governmental organizations (NGO) and
transnational terrorist elements as well. Each diagram and chart may
have connecting files to one or more others. They cannot be created
overnight and may not even be completed by the end of your tour; they
take time, patience, detailed patrolling, human intelligence, and reporting
and recording efforts. Your first reports and subsequent deductions may
be incorrect or incomplete - change the information as necessary.
Remember these are ***tools*** not products and serve only to shape
understanding, aid in planning and focus reconnaissance efforts. The
following examples are useful tools that can be adapted to match your
situation. The key principles of using diagrams and charts are readability,
adaptability and accuracy. Do not try to make a single diagram or chart

to fulfill all of your needs; limit the number as much as possible but do not sacrifice accuracy or readability for convenience.

- *Cell Diagrams*—The two principle diagrams are the "Spider Web" in *Fig 3-1* and the Umbrella in *Fig 3-2*. Both serve the same purpose and can be adapted as needed for differing situations.

Fig 3-1:

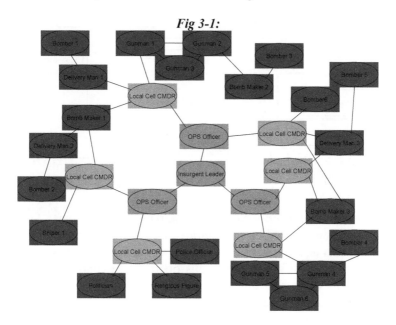

Fig 3-2:

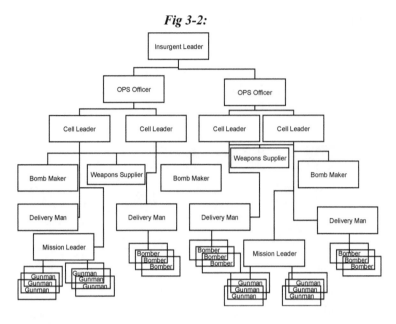

- *Network Diagrams*—Network diagrams can become far more complex and should be concentrated on known insurgents, suspected insurgents and key individuals in the community. They are excellent tools that identify both how cells operate and connections between insurgent networks, other organizations and key individuals (e.g. NGOs, transnational terrorists and political organizations). The example given in *Fig 3-3* is based off a cell lead.

Fig 3-3:

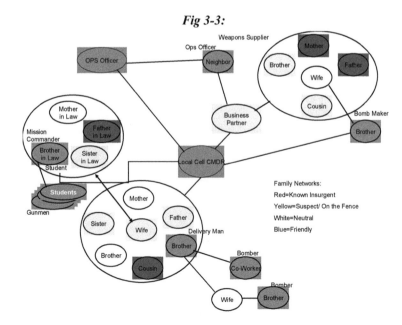

- *Patrolling and Movement Charts*—Patrolling and movement charts are used to schedule and plan patrols, record patrol activities and debriefs, identify insurgent and local patterns, and avoid pattern setting on your part. These charts contain cold hard facts, not deductions. You display only what is seen, heard or reported. The charts can be color coded and accompanied with spreadsheets; they are to be constantly updated and easily understood. *Patrol reporting charts* are used to track the activity of current patrols. They must allow for quick reads and easy tracking. The information on the chart should be frequently fed into an electronic database if you have the assets to do so. *Fig 3-4* is an example of a simple patrol reporting chart. *Mobility and Routing Charts* are used to identify patterns in friendly movement, insurgent movement and local schedules (e.g. times when the markets are busy, traffic jam times, etc.)

Fig 3-4:

DTG	Unit	Location	PIR*/**CCIR**/ Activity	Notes
151300 APR06	2/1/G	Café Leon, Russell Rd; Block H-5	**CCIR** Cell CMDR T. Freely seen meeting with known deliveryman P. Freely; money was exchanged.	Individuals departed area when patrol was seen. Patrol 200m from café observed through binos

NOTE: Use of specific location and **Unit Designated Grid System**

NOTE: Change ink color to identify importance of report.

Analyze, Plan and Train

Mission Analysis—The Marine Corps Planning Process (MCPP) templates are still very applicable in a COIN environment; in COIN however, the analysis requires more in depth information and broader consideration. Mission, purpose, end state, specified and implied tasks, and the development of courses of action are all factors in your study of the situation. In addition to traditional factors you must consider the cultural, economic, civil and diplomatic environment in which you are working, as well as the insurgents' *rallying message or single narrative.* Remember, the overall purpose is to mobilize the population behind *your message.* Use the information gathered in your Intelligence Preparation of the Operations Area (IPOA) to dissect the problem; the key questions you should look for are:

- What is the insurgency's main objective?

- What is their single narrative—their mobilizing message?

- What are the weak points in their message and how can you exploit them?

- What are the needs of the local populace and how can you gain their support?

- What is your message to the populace?

- How will you involve yourself with the local populace, and how will you pass and portray that message to the populace in your operations?

- What assets and contacts will you already have when you arrive?

- What will you need to request, build and develop to gain access to the locals and break down the insurgency?

Intent—What is the underlying purpose behind all of your operations? What are you trying to achieve? What is the one statement that will guide all of your junior leaders?

Concept of Operations—Make the plan simple and flexible and leave room for setbacks and changes. Unlike a conventional operation, there is no ground or single objective to advance on and measure forward progress. ***Remember the overriding objective is the support of the populace in order to marginalize the insurgents.*** There will be a constant ebb and flow of advances and setbacks of your goals as well as constant adaptations to your plan, tactics and techniques. Prepare for them now; do not allow your enemy to gain initiative due to a rigid plan and inflexibility.

The Message—Next, get the message that you need to send to the populace to mobilize them to your cause. Like commander's intent, this should feed from higher, and your *message or single narrative* should reflect the message sent from higher, aiding in the overall strategic objective. The wording and highlighted point must be specific to your area depending on the size and demographics of that area. Yours may be the exact same message as the division, regiment and battalion or it might be specific to the company; if your message does differ it should be approved and supported by your higher command. Utilize the minds of your junior leaders and, if available, an interpreter to ensure that the message translates properly and clearly.

Scheme of Maneuver—Again, the scheme of maneuver must be simple and flexible. Highlight by phase and be prepared to both move back and forth between phases as required and to have different units in different phases at one time. Also, no one phase or element can be a single approach; for example, security and dominance must be achieved immediately, however, that effort does not end once the goal is attained, nor should you try to gain security and dominance without simultaneously conducting civil, information or intelligence operations.

Wargaming the Plan—Bring in your subordinate leaders to try to predict setbacks and enemy weaknesses and to work out contingency courses of action (COA). Think through problems from the enemy's point of view and predict how they will react to your actions. Use a cunning and experienced individual to play the enemy against your plans. Then adapt your plan to stay a step ahead. Prepare to be wrong and adapt a step ahead of your enemy.

Task Organization

As you organize your unit take into account the key functions that have to be performed. Intelligence, information operations and civil operations are but a few of the issues that you may have to deal with on your own. Success in this fight comes at the small unit level, many of these tasks will have to be done together and many units will be doing similar tasks concurrently. Do not expect extra manning or aid from higher; prepare with what you have and expect minimal aid from your higher command. Give your most trusted leaders the billets that require the least supervision and give developing leaders the positions that can be closely watched. Listed below are some suggestions for task organization. Ultimately the decision is up to you; do not follow a single template; adapt your unit to best fight your area. An example task organization is presented in fig *3-5 and 3-6*, but yours must be adapted for maximum effectiveness in your own AO.

Intelligence—The insurgent is normally easy to kill but hard to find. Intelligence will become one of your main concerns and will require the majority of your time. Do not attempt to accomplish this task on your own; it is possible to form an intelligence cell at the company level. Put an officer, a Staff NCO or an NCO that is capable of performing detailed, complex and cognitive tasks in charge of this intelligence cell and support him with a team of competent personnel that can gather, sort and analyze information and make predictions about the enemy and indigenous personnel. *Key: Every individual within the unit is an intelligence collector.*

Operations Cell—It may also be necessary to establish a company ops cell to initiate and track plans. Counterinsurgencies are multi-dimensional and a company commander will be required to stay involved in every aspect; but not in every minute detail. Again, this is a consideration and it may not be applicable or even possible in your situation.

Information and Civil Operations—Information operations are central to mobilizing the populace. This cell should include a political officer whose sole job it is to provide you with information about the local populace. The perfect political officer is a State Department Field Officer that speaks the native language, knows the people and understands the culture. This may not be possible at the company level, but the billet is vital. A single officer or staff NCO must be assigned to this billet; the commander must have a constant feed of information and he should not attempt to do it himself, nor should he task it to his intelligence cell, which will be fully committed to the vital tactical information aspects of your operation. *Key: Just as every individual is an intelligence collector in COIN; they are also "transmitters" of our message to the local populace by his actions, conduct, bearing, and words.* Civil operations in most cases will be prepared and initiated by you and performed by another unit. Seek and be prepared to accept engineers and civil affairs personnel into your structure.

Translators—Translators are an invaluable asset. Set a precedence of where your translators will go when you get them and assign them to the intelligence cell for employment and control. Some translators may be Americans or Coalition personnel with clearances that have full access to all areas of your CP; however, in most cases they will be local nationals (LN) that must be kept away from sensitive information. **PRACTICE OPSEC!** Plan for living and accessible areas for your local national translators. Take care of them; they are more than just mouthpieces, they are direct ties to understanding the local populace and force multipliers. They are generally committed and highly responsive when made a part of the team and treated with respect. However, another consideration with LN translators is their existing prejudices. Many may come from tribes with long standing grievances with other local tribes; listen to their opinions, but take them with a grain of salt. Also, remember that your Marines / Soldiers will work with them daily; they will eat, patrol and even fight with them by their side and the bonds they form may be similar to the bonds formed with their fellow Marines / Soldiers. Inform and prepare your unit as to how to act with LN translators.

Operating Areas—A way to achieve a great deal of understanding of and connection with the area is to assign your subordinate units to their own operating areas. Let them become familiar with the streets, people and patterns of a specified area. The benefits are numerous: junior leaders can design their own patrolling plans with guidance, will have knowledge of the area, can develop trusted contacts and assets and can set their posture based off of their threat. This technique requires platoon commanders and squad leaders that are proactive, are able to grasp an understanding of changing situations and are capable of designing and executing logical plans based off of guidance. A set back of this technique is possible complacency and comfort with the area; this can be mitigated by proper supervision. Only under unusual circumstances should a commander shift unit operating areas because of the loss of area awareness and local relationships.

Functional Areas—A more centrally controlled method of task organization is to rotate units along functional areas. For example, one platoon conducts patrolling for a set number of days while another platoon is on guard and the third is on rest and QRF. This method gives units a break from the monotony and stress of a single task and can allow for more flexibility at the company level in some cases. It does not, however, allow for the same amount of contact with the local populace, nor does it allow for a detailed understanding of a specific area.

Attachments—Attachments are more than just increases in manpower and firepower. They are now a part of your unit, and you need to treat them as such. Be ready to employ them to the fullest extent of their abilities. Operational relationship will dictate the level of flexibility you have to employ your attachments and should be the first consideration when accepting them from higher. Examine their capabilities and how

21

you can use them; do not limit yourself to traditional thought or doctrine when planning for their employment; find out how they can best benefit the campaign and use them accordingly. Assimilate them as soon as possible, use their leadership to help determine capabilities and limitations and make them a part of your planning process. *Key: This demands that each unit have a coherent and rehearsed plan for integrating augments, be it an individual or a unit.*

Inter-agency Operations—Other government agencies are central to counterinsurgency. The State Department, national intelligence agencies, Department of Justice and Army Corps of Engineers are a few of the organizations that conduct operations in counterinsurgency. They are assets in conducting civil-military operations and it is imperative that you and they are working in coordination with each other. Train the company staff as well as a Marine per each squad on interagency operations. If possible set up briefings with their representatives and exchange your plan with theirs.

Training, Partnering and Advising Indigenous Forces—It is possible that you will find yourself working with indigenous military or police forces. These units are key to the eventual success of your mission. This task requires approval from the highest levels of command as it is a matter of national policy as reflected in the campaign design for the intervention in which you are engaged. Assuming you are directed to train host nation forces, there are some considerations for planning these activities:

- Determine the mission of the HN force you are training and how they will be used, and tailor the training appropriately.

- Avoid "mirror imaging" – which is the tendency to make the HN force behave and even look like you.

- Exercise great patience. The range of experience and the quality of HN personnel ranges widely.

- Focus on the basics. You may need to teach the HN personnel how to shoot and move as a team. Conversely, you may find the unit generally well trained and only in need of more advanced collective skills.

- Train the trainer. Where possible, you are usually served best by training a cadre of leaders within the HN unit and then assisting them as they teach their personnel.

- Using your small units as examples, show the HN unit(s) how to perform collective tasks such as day and night patrolling.

- Once a HN unit is basically trained, your personnel can act as an integrated training cadre to that HN unit. The next stage is coalition actions at the small unit level.

- Once a HN unit gains a measure of confidence from successful coalition operations against an enemy, they will be able to take on more demanding and complex combat tasks on their own.

- Treat the HN unit's personnel with respect—particularly their leaders. This engenders goodwill and should add to their confidence. This is especially true in the presence of the indigenous populace. You want them to believe in their security forces.

- You may have to work with the bureaucracy (or emerging bureaucracy) of the host nation in order to ensure that the HN unit you are working with is being paid and otherwise provisioned. Pay should come from their government—not you.

- If you plan to continue working with the unit, plan on posting a liaison team with the HN unit after you have trained them.

Fig 3-5: Example Company Task Organization

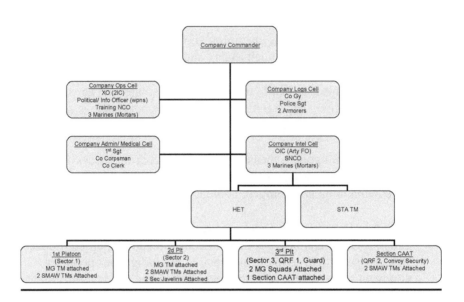

```
                          ┌──────────────────────┐
                          │  Company Commander   │
                          └──────────┬───────────┘
                                     │
   ┌──────────────────────┐          │          ┌──────────────────────┐
   │   Company Ops Cell    │─────────┼─────────│   Company Logs Cell   │
   │        XO (2IC)       │                    │        Co Gy          │
   │ Political/ Info Officer│                   │      Police Sgt       │
   │      (wpns)           │                    │      2 Armorers       │
   │     Training NCO      │                    └──────────────────────┘
   │   3 Marines (Mortars) │
   └──────────────────────┘

   ┌──────────────────────┐                     ┌──────────────────────┐
   │Company Admin/ Medical │─────────────────── │   Company Intel Cell  │
   │        Cell           │                    │      OIC (Arty FO)    │
   │       1st Sgt         │                    │         SNCO          │
   │    Co Corpsman        │                    │   3 Marines (Mortars) │
   │      Co Clerk         │                    └──────────────────────┘
   └──────────────────────┘
```

HET	STA TM

1st Platoon	2d Plt	3rd Plt	Section CAAT
(Sector 1)	(Sector 2)	(Sector 3, QRF 1, Guard)	(QRF 2, Convoy Security)
MG TM attached	MG TM attached	2 MG Squads Attached	2 SMAW TMs Attached
2 SMAW TMs Attached	2 SMAW TMs Attached	1 Section CAAT attached	
	2 Sec Javelins Attached		

Fig 3-6:

Port Area

Market Area

24

Training

Training and education must be ongoing activities – and you are the chief instructor. Develop a culture of training in which you prepare your unit members in advance of deployment, but continue to train even as you are executing in combat. Do this in such a manner that what you teach in training is practiced in combat and what is practiced in combat is borne out in ongoing (in-theater) training. To fight an intelligent and adaptive enemy, you must maintain the initiative of adaptation relative to your opponent, and training is your means of doing exactly that.

Teach and evaluate your junior leaders and company staff. They are your training cadre and they need to share your commitment to and philosophy of continuous training.

Where to Begin?—You will always have resource limitations to training. The time available to train during the precious weeks and months prior to deployment will come at a premium and you must focus on what is most important for your unit for mission accomplishment. Begin with what you deem the most important and work your way backwards to classes easily taught during down time in movement to theater. Backwards plan from your deployment date and include the battalion's training plan. Work with the S-3 and use the battalion's evolutions to reinforce your training. Ensure you use the training time to drive your mission and intent into your unit's psyche. The proper attitude and understanding of expectations cannot be overemphasized. Teach the ROE and ensure that Marines understand that it does not restrict them from self defense. Develop and solidify your SOPs, then base them against scenarios where Marines / Soldiers and junior leaders must make decisions. Follow with evaluations and remediation. Ensure that there is sufficient time in the schedule for subordinate leaders to train their units. You are the only one that can decide what training is most important to your unit and where the priorities lie. Focus on commander's intent, your mission and the unique qualities of your area and allow your junior leaders to do the same. Remember, however, that your higher headquarters will have a training program of which you are a part, and this will focus much of your training time. You must prioritize and make best use of every available moment in training. You must strive to train as you will fight.

Evaluation—Evaluation should not be prescriptive. Get to the root of why a Marine, Soldier or Sailor made his or her decision and adjust their perception of the situation. This type of process has three benefits: It builds confidence and proficiency in the junior leader's decision making ability. Your intent and expectations are continually reinforced. You may find that your intent may not be as clear or descriptive as you thought.

Company Staff—Remember that your reorganized company staff is doing jobs that most were not formally trained for. However, the value of education is that we teach our leaders to prepare them for circumstances that are beyond our ability to forecast. In this sense, leader education, formal and informal, enables junior leaders to bridge the gap between what the unit is trained to do based on what is known and what a mission actually requires. The best case would be to send members of your company team to formal schooling although this not often possible or practical. Set the standard for your team, put them in positions as soon as possible and train them using scenarios. When you go to the field establish a CP and have them perform their functions to the level of proficiency you expect. Push your intelligence staff to begin gathering and adapting your Intelligence Preparation of the Operations Area (IPOA), push them to brief the platoon commanders and coordinate with the other staff cells. Use your operations cell to start forward planning, executing and directing the other staff elements.

Attachments—Get your hands on your attachments as soon as possible, allow them time to train for their primary specialties and bring them into the fold. Train them with the rest of your unit, not as a separate entity. They must understand all of your SOPs and immediate actions. They must be as clear on your intent and expectations as the rest of your unit— completely integrated.

Leaders—Train your leaders to the point of complete trust and understanding. Evaluate the talents and abilities of your subordinates and assign them where they can best use their talents. Whenever possible, make them a part of the planning and decision making process. Give them the leeway to succeed. Supervise their actions and effectiveness and evaluate and guide them properly to high levels of initiative, mature decision making and a savvy form of aggressiveness.

Considerations for training: No list of training ideas can be comprehensive. Included below is a simple list to help leaders begin the planning process. A good view to adopt is to adopt a "patrolling culture" that treats ever action as a sub-set of mission accomplishment. These five rules form a basis for all of your preparation. Your attention to every detail in preparation must begin with your initial training and carry throughout every action.

- Practice pre-combat checks and inspections as an ingrained activity. Be exacting from checking eq1uipment to knowledge of actions on the objective. No detail is too small. These should be as common as brushing your teeth.

- Conduct rehearsals. The more you rehearse, the smoother your actions will be when action begins and the chaos of combat makes specific direction difficult or impossible.

- Conduct thorough confirmation briefs with all your unit leaders and take the time for a confirmation brief with all unit members before you begin your mission.

- Conduct thorough AARs. You learn from operations and adapt in advance of the enemy. Use AARs to help you adapt. Use wargaming to help your leaders learn from operations. Every scenario that you have war-gamed with your leaders will be a tool in their tool chest.

- Make post-action debriefs an integral part of both training and combat.

The "Big Three." Remember the "Big Three" rules when preparing for and executing operations:

- *Guardian Angels.* These are the alert Marines (or Marine), placed in ambush, unseen by the enemy, watching over their units. Your entry control point (ECP), patrol, squad, platoon, company establishes patterns by its very existence and movement. The enemy responds to those patterns and future expectations of patterns; no matter how innovative your tactics or silent your movement, eventually units are going to be spotted and a pattern of some type discerned by the enemy. You want to always have at least one Marine that the enemy can't find-at least one Marine in a position of ambush, overwatching the rest of his unit-alert, protecting-a guardian, ready to fire from ambush. Security is the first priority of work. Guardian angel placement is the first priority of security.

- *Geometry of Fires.* Active and continuous placement of units, Marines, and sectors of fire to ensure that, in the moment when fires are needed, the ability to fire is not masked by Marines or by innocents. This is a 360-degree fight, and your geometry of fires must take that factor into account in operations ranging from ECPs to snap vehicle checkpoints to patrolling alleyways to full-on urban combat.

- *Unity of command.* One Marine is always in charge. In the dynamic, nonlinear environment, with units all transiting through your battlespace someone must own the area of operations (AO), regardless of the rank of the senior interloper.

Standards and Ethics. These final five rules describe will help to form your unit's character and must be engrained in each unit member and every action.

- *No better friend, no worse enemy.* No better friend to the populace and no worse enemy to the insurgent.

- *First, do no harm.* Avoid and prevent the killing or wounding of innocents. This is inherent to our mission.

- *The people are not the enemy, but our enemy hides amongst them.*

- *Professionalism.* Our actions and appearance demonstrate our professionalism at all times. We are confident, alert, and proficient. We fully understand the nature of the fight, the rightness of our cause, and are ready to show our courage to those friendly and enemy observers watching our every move.

- *Consistent and continuous application of individual and small unit discipline and tactical skills.* These skills include use of micro-terrain, covering each other's back, understanding the value of cover and local security in relation to the enemy's ability to gain an advantage, and understanding that urban combat is all about angles. Guardian angels and alert leaders combine to create tactically cunning, hard to kill units. Complacency kills, and it only takes a moment of inattention for complacency to take its toll. Teach your Marines to be hard to kill.

CHAPTER 4

Mobilizing the Populace

As described in Chapter 2, insurgents use a variety of measures—coercive and persuasive—to mobilize the populace in support of their objectives. To succeed in countering the insurgency, security forces must also mobilize the populace so as to marginalize the insurgents, create a less permissive operating environment for their activities, and win popular support. Therefore the essence of COIN is a competition to mobilize the populace. This is not a new or "soft" approach. Marines like Chesty Puller have successfully done this in our history and it is vital to successful COIN operations. Popular mobilization can be conceived visually, as in Figure 4-1.

Fig 4-1

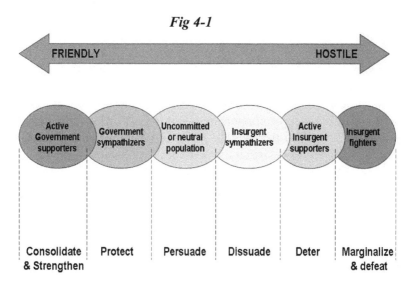

The populace includes a number of overlapping sub-groups, across a spectrum from active supporters of the COIN force to active insurgent fighters. The aim of populace mobilization is not solely to destroy groups at the "enemy" end of the spectrum, but also to progressively shift individuals and groups closer to the "friendly" end of the spectrum.

The enemy will try to force your Marines to hate all locals. Nothing is more critical to denying the enemy this victory than the attitude of sturdy small unit leaders who can combat shocks in stride and maintain their subordinates morale and fighting power. We are Americas elite and must never forget that we represent a great country that stands against oppression and evil. We must bridge cultural gaps and combat perceptions that distract from what we represent in order to undercut the enemy's support.

Purpose and Importance of Mobilization

The purpose of mobilization is threefold. First, it builds local allies that can actively or passively assist COIN forces in carrying out their mission. Second, it creates a permissive operating environment for COIN forces, improving operational security, reducing tactical friction, and allowing commanders to contemplate more ambitious operations than would otherwise be possible. Finally, it marginalizes insurgents, denying popular support to their activities, forcing them to spend more effort on force protection and security, and often causing them to turn against the populace – further exacerbating their loss of support.

Populace mobilization is fundamentally a political activity, and will normally be directed by civilian interagency leaders, primarily the country team under the U.S. ambassador, working in close cooperation with the military force commander and his staff. At unit level and below, commanders within the security forces work to support a broader set of political objectives designed to win over the populace.

Mobilizing the populace underpins all aspects of COIN. All operations, even logistic and force protection postures, or small-unit actions, affect the overall progress of political mobilization. And all operations, if mishandled, have the potential to undermine efforts to mobilize the populace. Every Marine needs to understand that his or her actions have strategic consequences in a COIN operation.

Populace mobilization is an incremental, gradual process. It occurs by *cementing* the support of local allies, *winning over* uncommitted members of the populace, and *marginalizing* hostile elements (insurgent sympathizers or supporters) within the populace. Large, spectacular, "quick-fix" activities rarely succeed in winning over the populace. A steady stream of incremental measures to build trusted networks normally works better.

Populace mobilization is primarily a matter of perception management –addressing the populace's expectations and perceptions to generate a desired effect. Perceptions matter more than reality in this context, and for the populace you are trying to influence—their perception is their reality. COIN forces must strenuously avoid creating expectations that cannot be fulfilled, leading to disappointment and loss of support. Commanders must constantly seek to understand and counteract rumors, popular misperceptions, and relationships with key community leaders.

Relationship to "Hearts and Minds"

Often the saying "winning the hearts and minds" is stated as a goal in COIN operations. Completely winning the hearts and minds is an unachievable endstate however, we are battling for support of the populace. Mobilizing the populace is a subset of "hearts and minds" activities. Hearts and Minds are two distinct but related areas of perception management, as follows:

- The "Hearts" dimension seeks to persuade the populace that their interests are best served by the COIN force's success. This is achieved by building a commonality of interest between the security forces and the populace, and giving the populace a stake in success. For example, development and assistance programs should be turned over to local community leaders, with the absolute necessary minimum of COIN force support – this allows the community to "own" these projects and feel they have a stake in the success of the counterinsurgency.

- The "Minds" dimension seeks to persuade the populace that the COIN force is going to succeed in its mission. This helps convince wavering community leaders to join the winning side, and deter those who might otherwise support the insurgents. It is achieved by demonstrating consistency, reliability and authority, building the prestige of the security forces and those who cooperate with them. For example, a visible security force presence in key populace centers, combined with public successes in arresting key insurgent leaders or defeating insurgent attacks, creates a sense of confidence in the populace. This must all be done while "maintaining the moral high ground" and keeping our honor clean.

31

Minimizing Alienation

All kinetic operations, particularly those that result in civilian death, wounding or property destruction, tend to alienate the local populace and reduce their support for COIN forces. This does not mean that such operations must be avoided – on the contrary, they are an essential part of COIN. Rather, commanders must apply force sparingly, seek to understand the effects of their operations on public perception, and act to minimize the resultant alienation. Key: Taken from the physician's oath, the guidance of "First, do no harm" has been used by the Marines. The concept is to recognize the local populace must identify that maturity, morality, and genuine concern abides with us, not the enemy.

Commanders must understand the process of alienation. Most commanders realize that popular resentment increases in the aftermath of a negative incident (such as an inadvertent killing of a non-combatant). But most incorrectly assume that such resentment gradually subsides after such an incident, until another incident occurs (see Figure 4-2 a). In fact, it is more normal for resentment to remain high after an incident or even increase, until the next incident raises it to a new high (Figure 4-2 b). Therefore commanders must have a detailed knowledge of the history of security force interaction with a given village, populace group or location in order to understand the degree of alienation and resentment in that area, and hence the amount of work required to win over that populace group. In general terms, when a populace has become alienated, only a concerted effort– usually working with and through local community leaders – will win back that populace. The mere passage of time or absence of additional "unfortunate incidents" will not suffice.

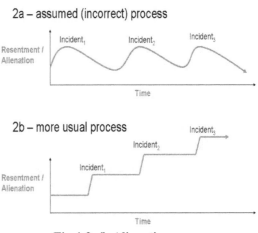

Fig 4-2a/b Alienation

32

Credibility, Honor and Reliability

Credibility—convincing the populace that COIN forces can and will deliver on promises made—is fundamental to mobilizing popular support. Credibility underpins the "minds" dimension of Hearts and Minds, by persuading the populace that COIN forces are serious players in the local environment. This is especially important for any promises or commitments given in relation to the populace's security. Commanders must follow through on any commitments made and, conversely, must avoid making any commitment that cannot be kept. The key is to avoid creating unattainable expectations and subsequent disappointment.

Honor is a major motivating factor in traditional societies. It is more important in tribal or remote environments than in settled districts and towns, but remains a prominent feature of any interaction between security forces and the populace. Commanders and troops at all levels must be sensitive to the honor of local community leaders, seeking to build the prestige of leaders who cooperate with COIN forces, while undermining the prestige of those who do not. Likewise, all members of the force must be sensitive to the issue of "face" – avoiding any incident that would tend to humiliate or undermine a local leader in the eyes of his people. Generally speaking, local community leaders will forgive mistakes, even those involving loss of life, far more readily than loss of face.

Reliability contributes to credibility by convincing the populace that COIN forces are a viable long-term partner. Periodic force rotation, every few months, makes it difficult for COIN forces to be consistent in meeting expectations and ensuring that commitments are honored. Commanders, planners and civil affairs staffs must conduct a detailed handover with predecessor units, to ensure that a complete record is kept of all such commitments. Commanders should also meet with community leaders as soon as possible on assuming control of an area, to ensure that their expectations are fully understood. In the event that commitments cannot be honored, keeping the populace informed of developments in a timely fashion can help reduce disappointment and thus minimize alienation.

Building Trusted Networks

A key element of IPB in counterinsurgency is an understanding of local networks within the at-risk society. Such networks include kinship ties, educational networks, economic linkages, patronage and influence networks, political party alignments, traditional trading or smuggling networks, criminal networks, ethnic and cultural groupings, religious networks and official government or state structures, among others. Commanders must enter their area with a basic mental model of these network structures, and a general plan to exploit them in order to build popular support.

Fig 4-3 Trusted Networks

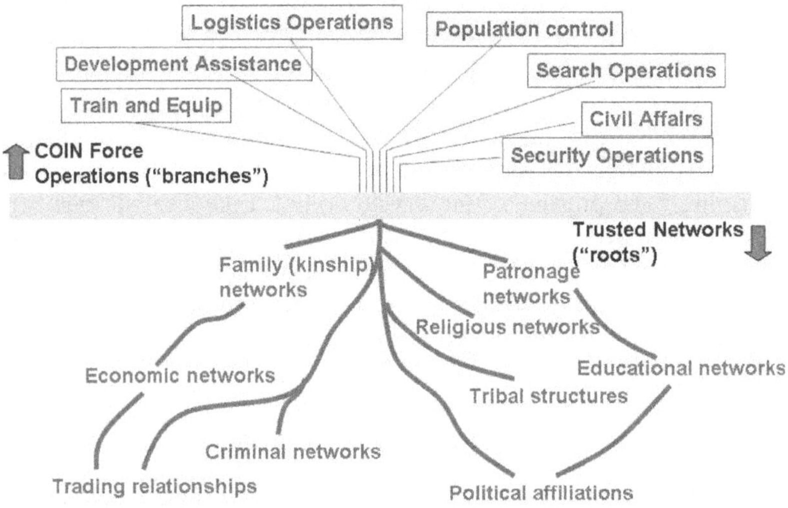

The purpose of building trusted networks is to create local allies, who share common interests with the COIN force and are prepared to act in support of COIN objectives while actively or passively opposing the insurgents. Such networks may be conceived of as roots (see Figure 4-3) which the COIN force puts down into the populace base. Like the roots of a tree, these provide stability and resilience in the face of setbacks. Also like the roots of a tree, such networks expand into the populace by following the natural line of least resistance. Finally, like tree roots, such networks require effort and emphasis; otherwise the whole campaign structure may become unbalanced.

One method of building trusted networks is to commence with local allies or supporters, then identify the key networks in which these allies operate. Targeted intelligence, civil affairs, liaison and security operations are then conducted to build bridges to other players in these networks, winning over further allies. The process is then repeated in an iterative fashion to consolidate networks of trust (Figure 4-4). Note that it is not necessary for the COIN force to interact directly with each member of a trusted network. Indeed, this may often be counterproductive since some members of the populace may be willing to cooperate with the COIN force's local allies, but not with the COIN force itself. Rather, at every level, commanders should seek to strengthen the position of local allies, and extend and cement relationships through them with wider networks.

Fig 4-4 Building Networks

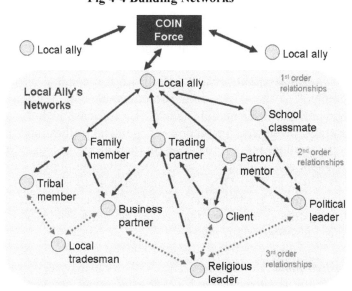

Methods of Mobilizing the Populace

Applying the concepts described above, the COIN force may adopt any or all of the following methods to mobilize the populace:

Physical Mobilization. Control over the methods and routes that the populace uses to move about the area assists in mobilizing popular support. Conducted properly, presence patrols, vehicle checkpoints and

35

security posts provide a feeling of security to the populace and allow commanders to influence their perceptions. Movement assistance (e.g. convoying or escorting civilian vehicles, providing transport for movement of goods to market, prevention of transport disruption, security of gasoline and oil supplies) also provides opportunity to build networks within the populace and win over uncommitted members of the community.

Psychological Mobilization. Mobilization of the populace through a range of psychological operations and influence activities provides leverage over key community leaders and groups. Activities should initially be directed to mapping the human terrain in the area of operations, identifying opinion leaders and influential groups and individuals. Once these are identified, influence operations should comprise two basic types: activities directed at securing the support and cooperation of key individuals, and activities directed at influencing the populace at large. Military Information Support Teams and tactical psyop teams are employed using similar methods as in other forms of warfare.

Political Mobilization. Political staff of the country team, the host government or the COIN force headquarters will direct activities in support of political mobilization. These may include support to registering of voters, protection of political rallies and canvassing activity, polling place protection during elections, support to local government administrators, intelligence activity to protect local political leaders allied to the COIN force, and support to electoral registration, vote-counting or election monitors. Close cooperation with interagency leaders is critical to ensure that troops' activities and posture supports established political objectives.

Socio-Economic Mobilization. The COIN force may support activities to mobilize the populace through developing social and cultural leverage via the trusted networks described in paragraph 6. Humanitarian and economic assistance, business promotion activities, reintegration and employment programs and support to commercial activity are key elements of socio-economic mobilization. Such activities are normally directed by Intelligence, civil affairs, aid and development and embassy political staff. Deployed units provide protection to key personnel conducting these activities, and provide a critically important stream of tactical reporting that enables commanders to assess progress in building networks.

Tactics, Techniques and Procedures of Mobilization

Needs assessments. COIN force commanders should develop a standard format for assessing populace needs, to include humanitarian, economic, development, security, health, education and environmental needs. Civil Affairs staffs normally maintain standardized survey questionnaires and other assessment tools, which have wide applicability as an intelligence and operational planning tool in COIN. All troops should be trained in conducting preliminary needs assessments, and in reporting assessment results to civil affairs staff and headquarters. Civil affairs staff must share needs assessment results with other staff branches via a consolidated populace database.

Tactical Reporting. All troops operating in a COIN environment – regardless of specialization – must be trained in tactical reporting of key populace indicators that allow staffs to assess progress in mobilizing support. Reporting guidelines must be jointly developed with interagency staff (especially political staff on the Embassy country team) and with civil affairs and intelligence personnel. Tactical reporting databases must be handed over to successor units and updated regularly as the situation changes – in particular, old reporting that is out of date must be weeded out. Village reports, route condition reports, records of conversation with key local leaders, infrastructure reports and economic activity reports are examples of some of the types of tactical reporting that may be established. All leaders, to the lowest level, must be aware of the importance of such reporting details and their role in keeping them up-to-date.

Inter-agency Operations. Deployment of health services, humanitarian assistance, civil-engineer, intelligence and psychological operations personnel in distributed small-unit operations may also provide significant benefits, particularly in urban areas with mixed populaces. This is a crucial aspect in gaining legitimacy for the local government authorities, who will have to remain and operate effectively once the COIN force withdraws. Cooperative police/military patrolling is a useful aid to interagency cooperation, but commanders should note that local police are not always accepted by the local populace – under certain circumstances the military or coalition forces may be perceived as more impartial. Where possible, however, arrests and interrogations of local community members should be carried out by police and include representation by local community leaders.

Inter-agency Operations Centers. Establishment of joint interagency tactical operations centers greatly assists in mobilizing the populace. Where feasible, these should include police, intelligence services, justice officials, aid and development officials, representatives of non-government organizations assisting in the COIN effort, Foreign Service political staff and coalition forces. It will not always be possible or necessary to include the full range of interagency representation at every level. At a minimum police, intelligence, military and local administration staffs should be represented.

Demonstrations. Demonstrations are a technique to assist in developing credibility and winning minds. These may be of significant benefit early in a tour as a "show of force". They may include staged events such as open days where the populace has an opportunity to understand the level of firepower, mobility and technology available to the force. More often, they will be impromptu activities where commanders seize an opportunity to impress upon the populace the COIN force's ability to assist the populace and hurt their enemies. Such activities may involve firepower and maneuver, but may also involve targeted civil affairs. For example, commanders may use forward teams to conduct a rapid needs assessment of key local villages, then follow these assessments with prompt assistance packages designed to show the populace that the government, through the COIN force, can respond to its needs. Again, while this can be a powerful tool, remember that an unfulfilled promise can be damaging to your credibility. The rule should be to under promise and over deliver.

Targeted civil affairs. Tailored humanitarian, medical and infrastructure development assistance, including provision of basic services, can be a significant tool in mobilizing the populace. Provision of humanitarian assistance must be grounded on human needs, but within these parameters groups that cooperate more fully with the COIN force can be targeted with additional assistance, greater financial and other incentives, and less restrictive security measures. Civil affairs teams working closely with intelligence staffs and commanders thus send a consistent message to encourage the populace to support the counterinsurgency effort.

Cyber-mobilization. Modern insurgents employ the internet and cell phone technology to mobilize supporters. In particular, the use of SMS messages via cell phone is a potent tool for rallying insurgent supporters, threatening government sympathizers, passing information and spreading propaganda. Because of this, commanders may allocate a portion of SIGINT effort to countering or exploiting SMS traffic, and a portion of psyop effort should be allocated to influencing the populace via SMS and internet. As with other forms of psychological operation, this technique is most effective when electronic means of mobilizing the populace are synchronized in mutual support with physical movement and maneuver.

Populace control. Populace control measures (including vehicle checkpoints, stop and search activities, cordon and knock, curfews, food and water control measures) are a potent tool for mobilizing the populace. They can be applied to produce incentives for supporting the government and disincentives for supporting the insurgency. Commanders may wish to divide their operational area into sectors, and grade each sector (e.g. a village or neighborhood) on its degree of cooperation with the security forces. Cooperative areas may then be granted additional privileges and incentives while more insecure areas are subjected to a greater degree of populace control. This approach is only effective if movement between cooperative and denied areas can be effectively controlled or monitored. Populace control measures are essential in COIN operations, but all involved must remain aware of the disruption to the locals, which can influence their perceptions of the COIN force. Marines must be "fair, firm, and friendly" when undertaking these control measures.

Locally-raised forces. As trusted networks and local alliances develop, commanders may be in a position to raise, train and employ locally-raised irregular forces. Such activity must always be coordinated with force headquarters and the country team in order to prevent the emergence of local militia outside government control. But provided local forces are loyal to local government leaders, they can be a useful tool in mobilizing the populace. COIN force units raise and train local partner units, normally keeping unit size small and equipment light and locally-procured. Local forces should be irregular in nature, operating in an auxiliary fashion in local areas. Besides providing a link to the local populace and improving situational awareness, such forces also provide a source of income for the community, prestige for local community leaders and additional leverage in building networks and help to put a "local face" on operations- thus enhancing local government authority and positively influencing populace perceptions of the COIN force.

CHAPTER 5

Information and Intelligence Operations

Introduction— Intelligence and information operations will make up the bulk of your unit's work. Every meeting, patrol, raid, arrest and civil action sends a message to the local populace, the insurgency and possibly the world; every observation, interaction and engagement feeds you with intelligence. Therefore, everything you do should intend to either gather intelligence or spread a message. They are the logic behind your operations and the means of mobilizing the populace.

Information Operations

The richest source of power to wage war lies in the masses of the people.
—Mao Tse-tung

The previous chapter discussed mobilizing the population in support of your efforts and away from those of the insurgents. Information Operations (IO) are the vehicle to achieve that end. Diplomatic, military and civil actions all have either a positive or a negative effect on the perception of your presence and should therefore be planned and executed with that effect in mind. Your actions must be justifiable and honest and your message must be consistent; you cannot please everyone, so do not try to. Many will be dissatisfied with your actions; the validity of your reasoning is the only defensive ground you will have to answer with. You will make mistakes. Be prepared to answer for them, maintain the moral high ground and make public restitution for public mistakes. Promise only what you can deliver, say what you mean and then do what you say. In the end, actions speak louder then words and you want someone to know about your actions.

Means of Dissemination—There are primary methods through which information spreads to the local populace, the host nation and the world. Whatever your aim or message, ensure that it is understood by all audiences; do not tell the locals one thing and the media another - the message should be the same for everyone.

- *Word of Mouth*—This is the most basic form of sending and receiving information, and ultimately the form that every other method will become. Word of mouth is the quickest, most common, most inaccurate and most uncontrollable means of disseminating information; but it may be the best way to send your message. Rumors, spins, casual conversations and dinner-table discussions — whatever form they take, word of mouth travels like wild fire. It spreads out of control and the story grows and changes with each conversation like school kids playing a game of *Telephone*. Everything your unit does is observed and discussed by the locals and spun by the enemy. Be sure that you are prepared to counter false information. Your patrols must interact with the populace. Listen for rumors and correct the ones you hear, but do not waste time arguing about them. Instead, stay positive, tell them the positive things you are doing, listen to their grievances and reinforce your *message.* You can also point out the negative effects the insurgency is having on them, however, do not direct it at a single individual or group unless your intent is to draw an argument; ties can run deep and you could offend your audience or worse, you could raise the perceived status of an individual insurgent and make him a rallying figure.

- *Announcements*—Both written and verbal announcements are quick and controlled means of sending messages. Flyers, loud speakers and public speaking are useful ways of informing the populace of progress, incentive programs, civil projects and operations.

- *Town Hall Meetings*—Town Hall meetings are an effective means of discussing points and counter points to your presence, operations and the unifying message. They tend to draw the people that are most interested in the issues and have the most legitimate grievances. This type of meeting also exposes the leaders of the community and the general opinion of the locals. These are planned meetings with an open forum. Use caution and do not allow yourself to fall into the trap of arguments that drag you down paths that are dangerous to your message. Keep in mind that it is an open forum and the insurgents will ensure that people sympathetic to their cause are present and are fighting for their interests in the political arena. A few considerations for Town Hall Meetings are:

    - *Get approval and interagency support.* This type of meeting requires approval from some of the highest levels; local government officials should be the main Chairmen of this meeting and you or a U.S. representative should be a board member. The U.S. State Department has a country team whose job is to develop relations with the populace and create a stable government. They should drive this campaign, get a representative from DOS involved as soon as possible to share in the planning process.

– *Choose your time, ground and topics.* Town hall meetings are not good tools when public opinion is already against you; however, they can aid in exploiting a rising following of your efforts. Therefore, the timing of such meetings should coincide with a noticeable rise in local opinion. Pick the place; ensure that you think through where you hold the meeting. Decide whether you want to hold the meeting in a pro-American or neutral part of the AO or if your cause has enough inertia to encroach on insurgent areas. Hold the meeting in a friendly area and you are telling the people, "Agree with us and we will help you." Hold a successful summit in an insurgent strong hold and you are telling the enemy, "Get on board because we are winning popular opinion." Choose the topics and stay focused, prepare for the perspectives of insurgent sympathizers and use your political officer and State Department representatives to keep you on track.

– *Prepare, Prepare, Prepare—Do not walk in cold.* Practice and plan; ensure that all officials meet prior to the Town Hall meeting and are on the same page. In every case be prepared to answer, as a group, the litany of questions and grievances that will arise. Know how to answer them—do not make promises you cannot keep and be sure that any other officials who attend understand that they cannot speak for your unit.

– *Security is paramount.* Gathering as a large group for any purpose provides a target for insurgents, especially one that could possibly challenge their ties to the local populace. In the best case, the base of security should be local, supported by advisors and reinforced with coalition forces. If people do not feel safe they will not attend.

• *Media*—The media offers a platform for both the host nation and the world. Television, newspapers and magazines circulate information, right or wrong, to a large audience. They can be biased and

43

sensational, and can help your cause or destroy it. Again, they cannot be controlled or manipulated however it is incumbent upon you to ensure they have access to your message and your actions. Reporters are professionals with experience in uncovering lies and relating to their audience. This can be the best opportunity you have to build support and let the world see what good you are doing; or it can be the worst enemy to your cause. The effect depends on how you treat the information/ media. Tell the truth; do not hide facts to try to protect your mission. If your unit makes mistakes, be honest with the people and let them know what actions you are taking to rectify the problem. Brief the media and give them access to what you are doing; sell your campaign, sell the human rights efforts you are taking and answer their questions honestly. Do not speak out of your lane; if you are a squad leader tell the reporters about your squad and what it is doing. Be prepared to speak with the media, consider designating an individual for that purpose. At the company level, one Marine should be charged with keeping contact with the PAO and coordinating media operations. Do not sell out your security; ensure that reporters understand your operational security requirements and let them know the rules as to what and where they have access. Once again, in the end your actions will speak louder than your words. Some media agencies will try to undermine your efforts; the majority of legitimate newspapers and broadcasters will report what they see and understand. Your job is to offer accurate information, protect sensitive information, speak only for yourself and your unit and do what you say you will do.

- ***Rules of the Road for Interacting with the Media.***

  - Don't divulge classified or details on updoming operations
  - Don't provide the enemy with insights to how we operate.
  - Don't give the enemy specifics on BDA or casualties.
  - Share your courage with the American people and the population you are helping, "No Fear"
  - Never grieve in public for a lost comrade.

Considerations for Information Operations—In counterinsurgency, IO is marketing; your operation is just like a new product that uses advertisements to make people aware of it. For people to buy it, it still needs to be a quality product. You are marketing your unit, your actions and your message to the local populace and, very likely, to the world.

44

- *Informational Objective* (What message are you sending in conducting a particular mission?)
  - Establish dominance
  - Create security
  - Establish rule of law
  - Achieve a tactical advantage
  - Provide a civil service
  - Remove a portion of the insurgency

- *Minimizing Collateral Damage*
  - What steps are you taking?
  - How are you ensuring this?
  - What are you doing to advertise this?

- *Control and Care of Civilians*
  - What control measures are in place to control onlookers?
  - How are you caring for civilians affected by your actions?

- *Control and Care of Enemy Captured and Wounded*

- *Means of Advertising*

Women—Women play an important role in counterinsurgency operations. There is a perception in many cultures that women are unapproachable and should not be spoken to by men, especially soldiers. You should recognize both the cultural protocol and the place women hold in the society. In many cultures they are trusted and respected members of the household and the population, therefore, women have a great deal of influence on the opinions of the family, tribe and village. Find out their needs and wants, which are often times based around their families' well being. Work to get them on your side and do not dismiss their opinion/ influence.

Intelligence Operations

Just as with information operations, intelligence gathering will span across all of your missions. This goes beyond Commander's Critical Information Requirements (CCIR) and Priority Intelligence Requirements (PIR). Gathering information on local movements, businesses, networks, cells, tribal disputes and business practices is essential to acquiring and maintaining your understanding of the situation and the area. You must continuously update your IPOA and cell and network diagrams. Each patrol you send out, regardless of their main purpose, must know what information is needed and must have specific information requirements to fill intelligence gaps. Every individual is an intelligence collector when trained and motivated properly.

Intelligence gathering is a continuous process and is accomplished through four primary means: reconnaissance patrolling, surveillance, human source intelligence and signals intelligence. Each form is effective and is complementary to each other. The following paragraphs present guidelines for using these tactics/ procedures.

Reconnaissance—Reconnaissance is the active search for raw information and is normally focused on search for specific information requirements. Some cases will require a clandestine team to conduct reconnaissance, but this is not always the case—overt patrols can, in some cases, perform the necessary tasks. In either case, units require a high degree of proficiency in communications, recording, reporting, patrolling, observation, photography and field sketching. Trained reconnaissance units are not always available so ensure that squads are prepared to perform these tasks. It is always possible to train a squad to perform such tasks. Reconnaissance patrols fall into two basic categories:

- *Area.* An area reconnaissance is a directed effort to obtain detailed information concerning the terrain or enemy activity within a prescribed area such as a town, ridgeline, woods or other features critical to operations. (Refer to MCRP 5-12C.) An area reconnaissance could also be made of a single point, such as a bridge or installation. (Refer to MCRP 5-12A.) An area reconnaissance is useful in acquiring details on a specific objective. A recon of an objective, a route recon and an HLZ recon, are all examples of area reconnaissance. Place importance on the required, detailed information; limit the scope but not the depth of raw information you require.

- *Zone.* A zone reconnaissance is a directed effort to obtain detailed information concerning all routes, obstacles (to include chemical or radiological contamination), terrain, and enemy forces within a zone defined by boundaries. A zone reconnaissance is normally used when the enemy situation is vague or when information concerning cross-country traffic ability is desired. (Refer to MCRP 5-12C.) The commander specifies routes or areas of interest within the zone. The zone to be reconnoitered is usually defined by a line of departure, lateral boundaries and a limit of advance.

Surveillance—Surveillance is a passive form of gathering information and is most effective when it is done in a clandestine nature. The range of tasks for a surveillance team can vary from observing a specific objective or individual to recording and reporting information about a street, neighborhood or area of interest. As with reconnaissance teams, those performing this task should be well versed in the disciplines of communications, recording, reporting, patrolling, observation, photography and field sketching. The teams should be small in order to remain undetectable with "guardian angels" maintaining over watch of their mission. Snipers are the ideal personnel for this task, however, it is advantageous to train personnel in your unit to perform this task as well. The methods of surveillance range from observation posts and hides to the use of personnel either mixed with the civilian populace or from the civilian populace to track and follow individuals, if the situation allows.

Human Source Intelligence—Gathering information from human sources, either from indigenous personnel, captured insurgents or third party witnesses can be the most effective form of generating intelligence. On the other hand, it can prove to be unreliable and incorrect. Both the Army and the Marine Corps have human intelligence personnel that are trained to develop sources and extract and analyze information from the population. Such personnel are valuable attachments even though every Marine or Soldier is a potential human source gatherer. Train your unit to talk with indigenous personnel and to record and report their findings.

Recording and Reporting—Recording and reporting the information gathered is vital to your effort as well as the overall intelligence picture. Develop systems to effectively and accurately collect and report information; if this is not a functional system even the best gathering plan can become insufficient.

- ***Debriefing***—Every patrol and contact must be debriefed. This paragraph gives examples and considerations for debriefings.

  - ***Considerations for debriefing:***

- Conduct the debrief as soon as possible
- The same select individuals should be charged with conducting debriefs.
- Segregate returning patrol prior to debrief
- Debrief the patrol as a whole—every member must be present.
- Have prepared debriefing questions
  - Begin with the honesty chart - trace the actual route taken *Fig 5-1*
  - Phase through the patrol from start to finish
  - As you talk through the patrol continually ask about time, weather, activity and key objects
  - Check on CCIRs during each phase and again at the end.
- The debriefer should allow the patrol members to "storyline" the patrol as well as allow them to expand on any information that sparks communication and recollection.

- *Considerations for processing debriefs*:

  - Times, routes and common occurrences are immediately charted (example of a Route Overlay *Fig 5-2*)
  - Debrief points and information are sorted and catalogued for analyzing on company intel flow charts
  - CCIR observations are reported immediately to higher
  - PIR observations and observations of interest are charted and reported to higher
  - All debrief sheets, tables and charts are data-based and backed up
  - Record points of particular interest and repeated occurrences in the company's daily log and transcribe them into the turnover binder
  - Consolidate the data so that it is easy to catalog and read—formatted paragraph reports should be summaries for commanders not working documents for analysts.

Fig 5-1:

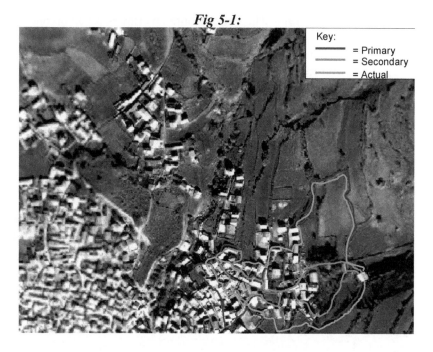

Key:
——— = Primary
——— = Secondary
——— = Actual

- *Recording*—Data must be recorded in an easy to analyze and easy to identify way, both in written and graphical forms. Your operations center should have posted graphs, diagrams, overlays and data-bases to allow your unit to see updates on the environment and the enemy. The intelligence cell should have backed up data-bases of information and update boards for Marines. The following considerations and examples are tools to aid you.

  - *Patterns*—You will need to analyze many patterns to develop a clear picture of the environment, and be sure the patterns you set ensure that you remain a difficult target for insurgents. You need to understand the patterns of the local populace; for example identify when they go to work, when the markets are busy and when the streets are clear to enhance your understanding of the area. The enemy will also set patterns; actions before operations, movement of supplies and frequent contacts are a few examples. Finally, your unit must avoid setting patterns such as times and routes of patrols and re-supplies and times and method of guard changes. In any case you will need a way of tracking these occurrences. The following are examples of possible tracking methods.

49

- *Route Overlay*—The Patrol Route Overlay is based on one of the routes plotted by the honest chart. This technique helps you find consistent choke points that patrols are crossing regardless of the original route. Once identified the canalized area is placed off limits for a period designated by the commander. *Fig 5-2* is an example of a Route Overlay, the 3rd patrol in the example is the actual route taken from *Fig 5-1* the other two are routes of other patrols that began with different primary routes.

Fig 5-2:

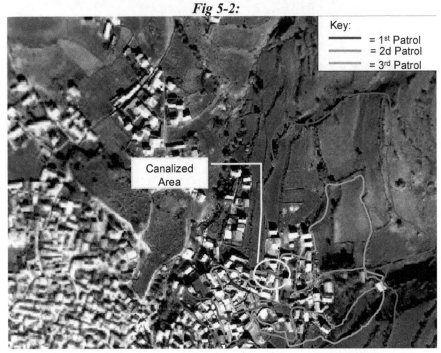

The Overlay is also used to determine common enemy routes. The example in *Fig 5-3* shows the reports from three separate patrols after enemy contact. The patrols all witnessed the enemy egress to the northwest; the next action taken was the company's emplacement of an STA team to observe the general area of egress. Subsequently, the snipers identify a particular house or area that the insurgents are occupying. With this information you can focus your gathering efforts and build your network and cell diagrams or your offensive operations. In addition, overlays can be used to determine key local lines of communication.

50

Fig 5-3

- **Key considerations for overlays:**
  - Focused—do not clutter the overlay; for example, instead of making an overlay for marked enemy movement, make one for enemy egress, enemy contact, enemy LOCs and "clam shell them" over the top of each other.
  - Mark reference points.
  - Use standardized formats that everyone is familiar with.
  - Use proper operational terms and graphics when applicable, but do not sacrifice the clear understanding of information for doctrine.
  - Continuously adapt it.
  - All copies should be made by the same personnel.
  - Color code (if possible).

Time Charts—Time charts help determine time patterns for you and the enemy and are good analysis tools to help determine the relation between your patterns and the insurgent's patterns as well. The examples in *Fig 5-4 to Fig 5-8* show a time chart and how it can point out the relationship between patterns. For example, in the diagram below, the pattern shows a gap in patrolling from the hours of 0100 to 0600 and an emerging pattern of enemy ambushes and IEDs from the hours of 0600 to 1200 and

1800 to 2100. You can also see that all of the arrests of possible insurgents occur between the hours of 0100 and 0600. One conclusion you can draw from this is that IEDs and ambushes are set in the early morning hours when your forces are not active in the area. You either confirm or dismiss this reasoning by considering other intelligence and by trusting your staff's and your own judgment. This data can then help you shape your intelligence and operational efforts.

Fig 5-4:

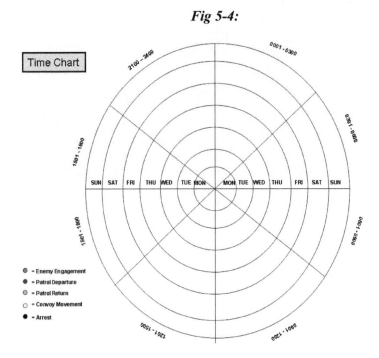

Fig 5-5:

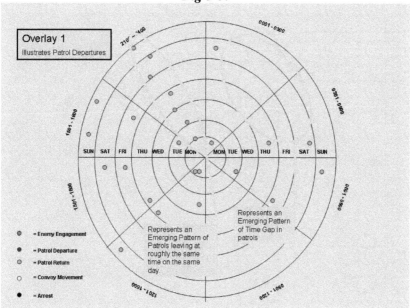

Fig 5-6:

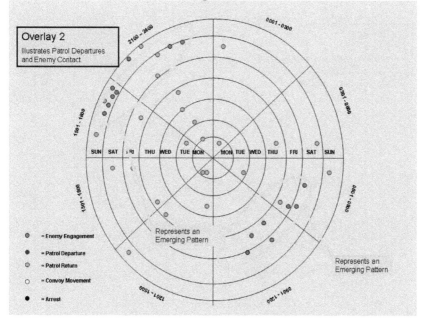

Fig 5-7:

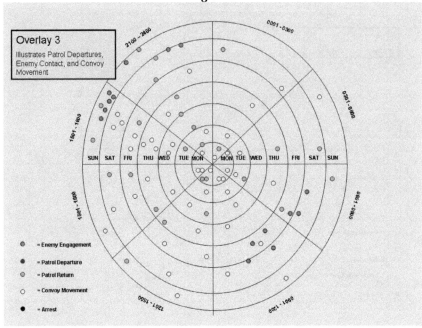

Fig 5-8:

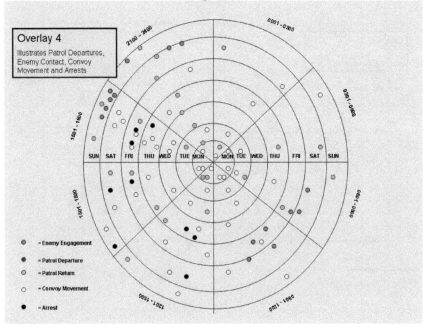

54

Long form reports—Charts and diagrams are great tools, but they cannot replace detailed analysis. This is the main reason behind dedicating capable people to focus solely on intelligence at the company level. To determine patterns and the intent of the enemy as well as the sentiment of the local populace, dedicated personnel must meander through tedious detailed reports and must continuously inform the commander and his operational unit leaders of any pertinent information.

Synthesis and Analysis—This is the most time consuming, detailed and tedious task in the intelligence process. Synthesizing and analyzing all of the raw information received from teams in the field, adjacent units and higher requires intelligent people educated on every aspect of the situation including sighting patterns and developing theories on the enemy's most likely actions, their relationship to the local community and their current disposition. Simply put, the synthesis and analysis process gives the commander the information he needs to make decisions on how to use his unit.

CHAPTER 6

Operations in a COIN Environment

To be effective in a counterinsurgency environment requires an eclectic mix of operations combined to achieve a common purpose. Chapter 5 discussed two of these operations, Information and Intelligence Operations, which are the two constant elements that cross all other operations. The ultimate purpose of everything, from building a school, to a raid, to the capture of an insurgent leader, is to both build the intelligence picture and mobilize the population in support of your goal. Every operation must be planned with the two former operations in mind.

Patrolling

Patrolling is the most versatile vehicle for conducting operations in a counterinsurgency. Just as in conventional operations, patrols are used to gain either a tactical or informational advantage over the enemy; in a counterinsurgency that advantage must relate to the populace rather than the enemy's tactical disposition. Each patrol has a purpose related to the mission; each patrol dispatched must contribute to mission accomplishment. No patrol is dispatched as a matter of course or routine. Constant patrolling is a necessity to establish presence and security; patrol bases must remain engrained with the local populace and the patrols themselves must engage with locals. Clandestine raids, surveillance and "Trojan Horse" type operations are also needed to verify HUMINT and observe enemy and local patterns in the absence of your forces. The effect of the patrol on the populace must be examined and weighed to determine the overall usefulness of the patrol. Success does not necessarily mean destroying the insurgent because this may lead to civilian casualties and collateral damage. Every decision must be weighed from the Company Commander down to the new private due to the possibility of negative strategic implications. The majority of all patrols' main objectives will be to collect intelligence and to show a presence within your AO.

Preparation and Organization —The knowledge and understanding of your AO will lead you to properly prepare for your next patrol. The organization of the patrol will be determined by the mission and commander's intent. Understand that your actions can have a detrimental impact on the bigger picture. Always remember that to defeat the insurgency, US and coalition forces must gain the support of the local populace. Acquire dominance immediately through your patrolling effort, get out among the people and face the insurgents as soon as possible; your actions or lack thereof will set the stage for your overall legitimacy and reliability in the eyes of both the people and the insurgents.

- *Preparation-* Preparation is the key for success and is required for every patrol before departing friendly lines. **All members must be present for the patrol order, rehearse, and know their role.** Pre combat checks to include knowledge of actions must occur. See Annex D. Confirmation briefs with the entire patrol present provide a good method to ensure that patrol members understand the mission, their role as well as the other patrol member's roles. Questioning not only the patrol leader but the individuals on roles and actions is a good way to build confidence. They must have an understanding of the possible threats to include location, method and nature that may be encountered on the patrol.

  - *Briefs and Orders-* Once the Patrol Leader (PL) receives the mission, conducts visual and or map reconnaissance and develops the plan using the six troop leading steps (BAMCIS), he can then issue the Warning Order (WO). The WO will be issued using a modified five-paragraph order as a checklist. After the WO is issued and the initial preparations are in progress the Patrol Leader begins his estimate of the situation (METT-T). Briefings and orders should include, but are not limited to, the following:
    - *Environment and Threats.* The intelligence brief will cover the operating environment, friendly forces, general and specific threats and suspect persons, vehicles and locations.
    - *IED/Mine Threat.* Commanders must make an IED/mine threat risk assessment for every patrol. The subsequent direction will affect off-road movement, 5 and 20m checks. All patrols must be informed of the IED/mine threat and the restrictions to SOPs that result.
    - *Operations Update.* The update should be given by someone from the operations center.
    - *Mission and Tasks.* Each patrol should have a specific mission and each patrol member must be aware of his/ her individual responsibilities.

58

5m and 20m Checks	
5m	**20m**
Identify a position to occupy. Carry out a visual check using Binos/optics, check for bricks missing from walls, new string/wire, mounds of fresh soil/dirt or other suspicious signs. Check the area from ground level to above head height.	The Patrol Leader identifies an area for occupation and stops 50m short of the identified position. The Patrol Leader carries out a visual check using binoculars then moves forward to 20m from the position and conducts a visual check using Binos/optics.
Before occupying the position carry out a thorough visual and physical check for a radius of 5m. Be systematic, take a little time and show curiosity. Use touch and, at night, optics.	The lead pair, with ECM Equipment, moves forward in single file to carry out an isolation circle of 20m radius from the center of the position to be occupied. Both observe and physically check the ground by zig-zagging across the circle. Remaining pair provide cover until the circle is cleared for occupancy.
Any obstacles must be physically checked for command wires. Fences, walls, wires, posts and the ground immediately underneath must be carefully felt by hand (without gloves).	

- *Patrol Routes, Alternate Routes, Check Points.* These points must be covered in detail.
- Individual and team sector responsibilities. This detail must be known by all patrol members.
- *Posture.* Soft or hard, depending on the task, situation and environment. The patrol posture may have to change several times during a patrol.
- *Immediate Actions.* These are likely to be SOPs but should be covered especially if there are local variations or new members in the patrol.
- *ROE.* ROE cards must be carried and understood.
- *Comm Plan / Lost Comm Plan.* Likely to be SOP but all should be briefed on what the plan is.
- *ECM Plan.* Likely to be SOP but all should be briefed on what the plan is.
- *Equipment distribution.* Equipment should be distributed evenly.

- **Medical.** Every Marine should carry his own First Aid Kit. Having a Corpsman on every Patrol is ideal but not possible in every situation. Ensure you have Combat Life Savers when possible/ needed.
- **Guardian Angel**—Every patrol must have overwatch. This begins with buddy teams watching each other and rises to sniper positions over watching the patrol and patrols supporting the sniper positions. The premise is to ensure that each unit is in mutual support of one another, everyone has someone providing security for them like a guardian angel making sure that no harm will come to them. This provides both security and psychological benefits.

- *Load.* Your unit's SOP should be developed to stipulate what load is to be worn or carried for the various types of patrols. The load will be linked to threats to, and posture of, the patrol and should be briefed to patrol members in sufficient time to enable proper preparations to be made. All patrols must have day and night capabilities regardless of the expected duration of the patrol. You must take into consideration the mark or footprint that you are making in your AO. How can we work towards gaining the support of the local populace? Do we have 2 MG Teams, 2 SMAW Teams per patrol and AT4's for every Rifleman or do we take minimal gear and have a beefed up QRF?

- *Equipment.* Equipment carried by the patrol will be environment and task specific.
  - **Radios and ECM equipment.** Radios and ECM Equipment should be checked at the point of issue prior to every patrol to ensure that the equipment and ancillaries are serviceable and operate correctly. Sufficient batteries must be taken for the duration of the patrol. Patrol members must be competent in the operation of all ECM and radio equipment. It is the commander's responsibility to ensure that radios and ECM equipment are switched on and working and communication checks are conducted prior to leaving the base location.
  - *Weapons.* All weapons must be prepared for firing prior to departing friendly lines. Slings must be used to ensure weapons are not separated from their bearer were he/ she to

be incapacitated and to allow the weapon to be slung when required.

- **Ammunition.** Sufficient ammunition and pyrotechnics must be carried to enable the patrol to conduct its mission.
- **Daypack.** Patrol members should pack their daypack with sufficient personal and team equipment to enable them to be retasked (e.g. manning a cordon, VCP) without returning to the Patrol Base. An SOP should be developed to detail the daypack contents (e.g. 48 hour rations, sleeping bag, radio batteries, etc.). Daypacks should be held by the QRF or Company Gunnery Sergeant, if not carried by the patrol, to facilitate delivery to the deployed patrol.
- **Documentation.** Patrol Leaders are responsible to the Platoon Commander for ensuring that appropriate documentation is carried by individuals for the conduct of the mission. Troops must carry their ID Card. A number of equipment checks should be conducted prior to the patrol.
- **Individual Equipment Check.** It is the responsibility of every patrol member to check his or her individual equipment. Marines should ensure any loose items or equipment are secured to the body or kit, including notebooks, flashlights, etc. Mission critical items are the only items that should be carried/ worn.
- **Fire Team Leaders Equipment Check.** Commanders must ensure that individual team members limit what they carry other than what is required for the patrol. Team equipment must be checked for serviceability.
- **Patrol Leaders Equipment Check.** Patrol leaders should check random items of individual and team equipment from each team prior to deploying, taking particular interest in the serviceability of mission specific equipment.

- **Rehearsals.** Patrols should rehearse immediate action drills, and drills for exiting and entering the security force base location.

- **Communications Check.** Communication checks should be conducted with the Ops Room before every patrol. Patrols should not leave the security force base until all communication systems have been proven to work.

– *Checking Out.* Patrols should check out with the Ops Room before exiting the base location.

- *Patrol Organization.* After studying your IPOA checklist, obtaining an understanding of the area as a whole and receiving your mission you are ready to organize your patrol. One must think outside of the box and use innovative ideas and tactics. The general organization would include the Patrol leader, Assistant Patrol leader, Navigator, Radio Operator, Corpsman and any attachments or detachments. All Marines should be proficient in many of these areas to provide flexibility for the PL. You will still need to have the assault, security and support elements but the footprint will be smaller and the coordination must be better. The following are some examples of what attachments you may need:
  – Interpreter
  – Police (MPs or local)
  – Specialist Search Teams
  – Females
  – Dog and dog handler
  – Demo Team
  – Sniper Team

- *Principles of Patrolling*—When preparing for and during the execution of any patrol all members must consider and use the principles of patrolling. There are not many changes from one environment to the next but in the Urban/ COIN environment your situational awareness must be at a high state of alert.

  – *Mutual Support.* Mutual support while patrolling is achieved by coordinating the movement and actions of teams while, at the same time, taking into account weapon/ECM/Communication capabilities and ranges. The wedge formation allows at least two teams to react to an incident involving the third team. Mutual support during contact is generally provided by the out of contact teams attempting to move 100-150 meters into the depth of the firing position. The team in contact must provide sufficient information to allow positions of mutual support to be adopted by the other teams. Satellite patrolling is another means of generating mutual support while covering a larger area.

62

- *All around defense.* Each team can achieve all around defense by overlapping fields of fire within each team and squad; within a patrol, teams can be assigned fields of fire to provide all around defense.

- *Separation.* Physical separation between teams makes all around defense for the multiple teams difficult to achieve. All around defense, when moving through choke points or higher threat areas, should be planned and rehearsed prior to commencing the patrol. When static patrol tasks are to be conducted, one third of the patrol should adopt fire positions covering the remainder.

- *Depth.* Within a team, and at multiple levels, depth is achieved by adopting a pattern of mutually supporting positions within the ECM umbrella. Depth is also achieved by using other deployed or static security forces, including police, QRF and air support (rotary, fixed wing and UAVs). The distance between each team on patrol should be influenced by the extent of the patrol route and adjacent patrols/ units.

- *Deception.* Deception should be employed to introduce doubt into the mind of the insurgent as to the purpose, route and activities of the patrol. The insurgent will look to predict the actions of the patrol so that he/ she can either target or limit the effectiveness of the patrol. Insurgents will look to establish patrol patterns so they can mount an attack at a time and place of their choosing. If the actions of the patrol are unpredictable, some insurgents will be deterred from mounting an attack as there is a higher risk of discovery and/ or capture. Some methods of achieving deception on patrol are as follows:
  - *Change exit and entry drills*, including utilizing mobile pick-up and drop off.
  - *Change patrol formations and numbers*, including the structure of a multiple. For example, varying multiples between 2 teams of 6 Marines and 3 teams of 4 Marines.
  - *Vary patrol routes.*
  - *Avoid pattern setting* (doubling back, mobile lift and drop).

- *Communications.* The communications plan must be robust and communications must be maintained throughout the patrol.

Every patrol member must understand the lost communications procedure. Without communications a patrol or a team within it becomes extremely vulnerable. Communications enable the Ops and Commanders to keep the patrol informed of threats and intent. Every patrol member has a responsibility to keep the remainder of the patrol informed of anything noteworthy, including observed changes in normal behavior among civilians, suspicious activity or even a lack of activity.

– *Counterinsurgent Tactics.* Patrol members must remain vigilant and suspicious. Insurgent activity has to be planned and prepared; the signs are visible. Patrol members should be encouraged to question whether what is seen is what it appears to be (turned up dirt, dead carcasses, no civilian activity, etc.). They should be skeptical and reluctant to accept things at face value. Reporting suspicious activity, lack of activity and things that are abnormal to your AO contribute to the development of a low-level intelligence picture, help achieve mission success and can save lives. Patrols must not set patterns; to do so is to invite attack. Vehicles must not stop at the same locations and Marines must vary their firing positions and the cover they use when static. Patrol activity must be unpredictable; routes and timings must be varied.

Civil-Military Operations

Whether supporting Civil-Military Operations (CMO) or actually conducting the CMO with organic forces, make sure that civil affairs will become a part of your daily operations. CMO is a major element in your relationship with the local populace, and to be effective, the tasks you undertake must be relevant to the locals. One of the mistakes made when conducting civil-military efforts is rushing into an effort without understanding the needs of the local populace; in the worst cases units make promises beyond their capabilities and scope. Building, governance, economic stimulation and medical support are a few examples of how broad CMO can reach. In any given theater of operations several organizations can aid in your efforts; USMC and US Army Civil Affairs units are your main ties to conducting and coordinating the bulk of your civil actions. On many efforts USAID and the State Department's Office of Reconstruction may be involved in your area of operations. Regardless of the agencies involved, this is your AO and you must stay involved with all upcoming and ongoing efforts. Remember, you are the one that will have to live with whatever happens in your AO, everyone else is just a tourist.

Considerations for Planning

- *Identify the problems*—Each area has different needs. For example, a city with a large amount of children may require that a school be constructed or rebuilt. Perhaps there is no city governance to organize, plan and represent local needs or perhaps the poor sanitary conditions require better waste disposal methods. A small agricultural village will probably have little need for a school or an organized government; rather, they may be more concerned with drinking water or an irrigation system. If someone comes and builds a school in that rural community it will have little practical use and will most likely offer you little success in gaining local support. Spend time observing the area, speak with the locals, understand their needs and act on them. Inform your higher echelons and other agencies of their needs and actively seek aid in meeting them.

- *Promise less then you can deliver*—Do not lose sight of the fact that you are still in an armed insurgency. What you are capable of is adulterated by the enemy situation. Supplies, workers and other operations are going to have an adverse effect on what you can accomplish in a single period of time. WHATEVER YOU SAY YOU WILL DO, YOU MUST DO. Not completing a task is a poor message to send about your reliability.

- *Start small*—Begin with projects you can affect directly and immediately. A series of small wins now is better than one big win two years from now. You must show that you are proactive immediately. The effort can be as small as building a bus stop or arranging for cleaning up trash on the streets; anything tangible that is needed and can be done relatively quick. Just as you would continuously improve your defensive position, continuously improve your AO.

- *Coordinate with interagency and Nongovernmental Organizations (NGO)*—Other organizations conducting civil operations in your area can become enhancers of your efforts. Keep in mind that you do not control these elements but you are all working toward similar

65

goals; coordinating with each other can truly aid you in shaping your effect on the situation.

- *The marketing plan*—It is not enough that you are helping the community - if no one knows about it then it may as well not ever have happened. Your enemy will take every opportunity to degrade your efforts or take credit for them. The information battle is the one you must win.

- *The intelligence plan*—If there are Marines or Soldiers in contact with civilians, they are sensors. Every operation, meeting and observation is an opportunity to understand the people, the environment and the enemy.

- *Layered plan*—Your plan should be layered as short term, mid term and long-term efforts. Use the short terms for the *quick wins*, the mid term sets the stage for self-reliance of the host nation and the long-term plans should provide a workable infrastructure for the host nation.

Conduct of CMO

- *Security*—It is almost a given that your enemy will attempt to derail any effort that gives you positive access to the civilian populace. Proper security is necessary to ensure success. The *Guardian Angel* concept is continuous. All civil activities must be supported by both passive and active security measures. Guarding the general area is not enough; an aggressive patrolling effort must be maintained. Snipers or designated marksmen in clandestine positions can provide over watch and local police or military can provide excellent cordon and check point forces. The enemy may also take advantage of the situation to move freely through normally patrolled areas that are vacant due to the focus on site security. Use economy of force, and vary patrol routes to ensure that you maintain presence in the remainder of the AO while maintaining a QRF to back them up.

- *Work with the locals*—Use locals to perform tasks when possible and pay them properly. This can help to regenerate the economy, relationships, security and intelligence.

- *Collect and debrief*—Gather as much information as you can. This is an excellent opportunity for interaction and gathering information from a different perspective. Have Marines or Soldiers assigned to interact with the people and NGOs, build contacts and draft reports. Debrief all military and government personnel that are involved with the effort daily.

- *Inform everyone*—Tell higher and adjacent units about your actions, progress and perceived results. Let the media in, let them see what you are doing. Be proactive in informing as many news organizations as possible about all of your actions. Arm your patrols with information about the different projects and have them discuss those projects with the locals they come in contact with; try to get a sense of the public perception from your patrols. You are advertising consistent progress, fueled by your unifying message.

Security Operations

Security Operations refers to the security of the local populace and it is essential to ensuring your ability to operate freely and remain legitimate as you conduct other operations. The inability to dominate the enemy will elevate their status and weaken yours. Public order, aggressive patrolling and foreign internal defense are all means to creating a secure environment. As we examine the considerations of conducting these actions keep in mind that this is all relative to the accepted norms of governance, freedom and culture. You will not create an American culture in an unstable environment. As with all operations, *security perations must support the overall information and intelligence effort.*

Kinetic operations

- *Patrolling*—Constant presence is the best way to ensure contact with the enemy at the right time. Patrols must be ubiquitous and when confronted with enemy contact; they must dominate the situation while incurring as little damage as possible to the civilian populace and infrastructure.

- *Assaults and Raids*—Assaults and raids must be precise, limit collateral damage and provide an informational purpose. They are not meant to simply degrade the enemies' combat ability, but to display dominance and eliminate well-known threats. Conduct assaults and raids with discretion and with exact precision. Destroying the wrong target at the wrong time can destroy your effort to mobilize the populace and stop the insurgency. An excellent example of this was a helicopter assault on a high level meeting between Adied's Lieutenants in Somalia; the participants gathered to discuss advising Adied about working with U.S. forces. The assault itself killed several civilians as well as any hope of communication between security forces and the warlord. In the end, this tactical victory led to a strategic loss.

- *Snipers*—Snipers are invaluable assets in this environment. They can destroy targets with no collateral damage, observe and report actions without the enemy's knowledge and make well-educated decisions based on the situation and intent given to them. Little will keep an enemy in line more than the knowledge that at any place and time he may be observed and targeted.

Public Order Operations—Public Order (PO) operations involve security forces managing, containing and dispersing groups and crowds of civilians intent on confrontation or violence in order to achieve specific ends. Responses to incidents of public disorder vary from tolerance, escalating through riot control, to the use of lethal force for the protection of human life.

- *Principles of Public Order Operations*

  - *Preventative Approach.* A de-escalatory attitude should be adopted to prevent incidents of disorder. Attempt to stay non-adversarial, non-kinetic for one day longer, one minute longer, remembering we're trying to win the goodwill of the populace, even when it appears doubtful. **Key: Remain prepared to apply decisive, precise firepower but it is not the default approach—"No better friend, No worse enemy!"**

  - *Mission Focused.* Troops should resist becoming embroiled in civil disorder that does not relate to the mission.

  - *Balance.* Commanders must deploy with the means to restore a situation should violence break out. In PO operations, numbers create a significant advantage. To this end, PO operations carry with them high human resource and equipment requirements;

anticipation will be vital if adequate resources are made available.

– *Flexibility.* The force posture should be changed according to the situation.

– *Communication.* PO operations are fundamentally about dealing with people. To this end, commanders must be prepared to negotiate with community representatives who may be able to positively influence the crowd's behavior and perception.

• *Employment of Military Forces in PO Operations*—Military forces can be deployed on PO operations in support of the police or when the police presence is either unavailable or incapable of primacy.

– *In Support of the Civil Police*—The deployment of military forces on PO operations in support of the police assumes police primacy:
  ▪ *Planning will be joint.* The police will state the resource requirement and overall intent of the operation.
  ▪ *The police will place themselves at the point where confrontation is most likely.*
  ▪ *The police will have responsibility* for the maintenance, preservation and, when necessary, rebuilding of relationships within the community.
  ▪ *The police will lead in the management* of, and interaction with members of the crowd, including appointed marshals and community representatives.
  ▪ *The ROE on the application of force by Marines will be broadly similar to those for the police force.*

– *In the Absence of Effective Police Presence*—The deployment of military forces on PO operations in the absence of an effective police force may arise when the civil police have lost control of disorder or when operating in a state where law enforcement institutions do not exist, are discredited, or have collapsed. Such deployments carry with them the following implications:
  ▪ *Military forces are likely to be responsible* for relationships with the local community, its representatives, and for crowd management. This requirement is likely to have to be met

against a background of poor intelligence and language barriers.

- *Military forces will be constrained by international law and* the need to apply reasonable and proportionate force.
- *Military forces may be able to use equipment and tactics that would be considered politically unacceptable under normal circumstances* (such as the employment of armored vehicles).
- *A breakdown of law and order will require military forces to be able to withstand a much higher intensity of violence* (including a substantial lethal threat) than would be expected of a civil police force.
- *The level of force necessary will be governed by the need to preserve life and prevent serious injury.* This may require the application of lethal force against rioters in appropriate circumstances.

- *Spectrum of Public Disorder*—Public disorder ranges from increased tension in the civil community to rioting resulting in the loss of life. Public disorder can escalate and de-escalate rapidly but will generally follow a number of identifiable steps as represented by the diagram in Figure 6-1. Any number of escalatory and de-escalatory changes may take place during a public disorder incident and the violence threshold may be crossed a number of times during a particular incident. Alternatively, the violence threshold may never be crossed or might be crossed very rapidly after an incident arises. Remember that the enemy may attempt to use a public order incident to draw us into over-reaction by inciting the crowd or using them as a tool for their own operations against us.

70

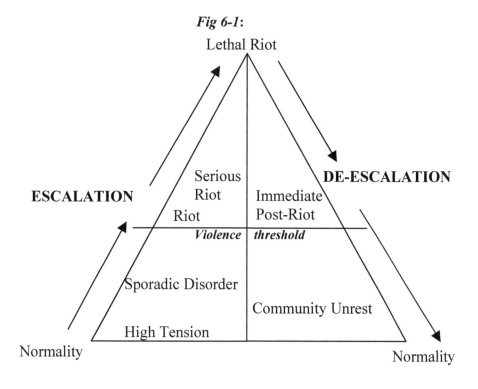

Fig 6-1:

Lethal Riot

ESCALATION   DE-ESCALATION

Serious Riot

Immediate Post-Riot

Riot

Violence | *threshold*

Sporadic Disorder

Community Unrest

High Tension

Normality   Normality

- *Changes to Force Posture*—The posture of the security force should change in direct proportion to the level of crowd violence. The crowd should always be seen as the aggressor. The response of troops to any given situation is the responsibility of the commander who will order changes to force posture as required. Changes in force posture may result in changes to equipment carried and used. It is possible to use a baton and/ or shield in such a way as to cause fatal injuries. A shield and baton may only be used to strike a person with lethal force if he/ she is committing or about to commit an act likely to endanger human life and there is no other way to prevent the danger. The commander of the security force at the scene or his representative should issue a warning to the crowd prior to the use of public order equipment unless:

  ▪ *To do so would increase the risk of death or serious injury* to members of the security force or any other person other than the persons committing violent disorder.

71

- **The security force personnel in the immediate vicinity are under armed attack**

- *Crowd management*—Incidence of crowd violence does not imply that the situation is irreversible. Careful management, situational awareness and communication may allow de-escalation below the violence threshold which may enable the restoration of order. Our goal is de-escalation of violence. We are fighting for the goodwill of the populace our actions must be guided by a respect for their needs. However, we remain prepared to deliver timely and precise firepower if required. "No better friend; No worse enemy." Understanding the local area, its geography and demographic make-up and the wider political situation will assist commanders in identifying potential flashpoints for public disorder. Local intelligence, including combat indicators from patrols, can often provide early warning of crowd events. Commanders must be prepared to listen to community concerns and should establish liaison with community and tribal leaders whenever possible. The following process can be used to assist in identifying who will be most helpful in influencing the community:
  - *Identify Stakeholders*—Identify those who may have a stake in a forthcoming crowd event. Stakeholders may include shopkeepers, street vendors, religious leaders, tribal leaders, civil leaders, local Police, and / or business representatives.
  - *Identify Suitable Representatives*—Once stakeholders have been identified a filtering process must be conducted to identify those stakeholders that are appropriate to act as intermediaries between the security forces and the crowd.

- *Facilitation*—Security forces must consider whether a gathering is legal or illegal as it will influence the force posture and method of interaction with the crowd.

- *Illegal Crowd Events*—Security forces should refrain from adopting a black and white approach to an illegal crowd event as to do so will often result in confrontation. The riot that follows a robust attempt to uphold law and order by the security forces will cause damage and distrust that may far outweigh and outlast the often transient impact of the law-breaking activity. In some circumstances, it may be better to allow illegal crowd activity

72

(particularly noisy, but non-violent demonstrations or protests) to continue unchecked in anticipation of the crowd dispersing. Commanders will have to weigh the risks inherent with the deployment of public order troops against allowing minor criminal activities, such as looting, to continue. (Looting may not be as damaging as the wholesale destruction of the street during a riot.) Credibility of the security force must also be considered and illegal activity can not be allowed to escalate unchecked. Commanders must use common sense when responding to illegal crowd activity.

- *Legal Crowd Events*—When crowd events are legal, the security forces must do all they can to assist the members of the crowd and their nominated representatives. The community, and thus the crowd, must assume responsibility for its own policing whenever possible. Where relationships have been established with effective community representatives prior to the event, steps should be taken to ensure the appointment of stewards or marshals from within the community. In the absence of established relationships with community representatives it may be necessary to enlist the assistance of those who have influence over the crowd as they are identified. During legal crowd events, the security forces should adopt the softest possible posture towards the crowd. The attitude of the security forces should be one of facilitation rather than confrontation.

- *Communication*—Poor communication and associated misunderstandings can enhance any grievances and result in confrontation. Interaction with the crowd and with community representatives will identify issues that need clarification. Commanders must try to identify and manage false expectations and facilitate the passage of information to the crowd via its representatives

- *Legitimacy*—The security forces will gain legitimacy in the eyes of the crowd if they can be seen as acting reasonably. As long as possible, people in the crowd must be treated and addressed as individuals. If security force actions are not lawful, proportionate and disciplined, then credibility will be lost along with any ability to influence other than by/ with the threat of force.

73

– *Balance*—There may be hostile elements that have a vested interest in provoking a riot. Crowd violence may be inevitable, regardless of the security force posture adopted. Commanders must retain tactical balance throughout a crowd event. Specific considerations include:

  ▪ *Prevent the isolation or separation of elements of the security forces by the crowd.*

  ▪ *Have a robust extraction plan* for the security force elements in soft posture whose task is interaction with the crowd.

  ▪ *Have a reserve trained and equipped* to stabilize a violent situation and enable the extraction of troops who are insufficiently equipped for the situation. The reserve should be a minimum of a sub-unit, which should be kept out of sight of the crowd but in a location where they can be employed at short notice.

• *Crowd Management Techniques*—There are a number of crowd management techniques that can be employed by the security forces including:

– *Reducing the Size of the Crowd*—A crowd will be easier to manage and is less likely to become violent if it is smaller and does not perceive that it carries a substantial numerical advantage over the security forces. The crowd around a specific point/ event should be minimized. Two techniques can assist with this process:

  ▪ *When the timing and structure of an event is within the control of the security forces, consideration should be given to staging a number of small events consecutively over time rather than one mass event that may draw a large crowd.* An example includes the distribution of food to specific discrete areas over a week, rather than running a single district food point. In such cases it is vital that the prospect of later distribution is credible and liaison with community representatives will be critical to maintaining credibility.

- **Filtering and Screening.** The crowd should not be allowed access or view of the focal point of a crowd event when possible. Filtering and the careful positioning of screens will assist with this process. The filtering process must be seen as fair and impartial. Credible community representatives can assist with this. In addition to denying the crowd the opportunity to rush the focal point, filtering and screening will serve to discourage the viewer groups who make up the majority of any crowd. The crowd will thus be substantially smaller.

- *Queuing and Waiting*—A crowd will naturally wait around if they perceive that there is a benefit in doing so. Organizing the waiting crowd into a queue can be a challenge and is an activity that should be conducted with minimal confrontation. Of critical importance to the members of any waiting crowd is an understanding that, by conforming (i.e. queuing), their turn will come. Tensions will rise quickly (and understandably) if the reward is denied to those who have waited several hours in anticipation. Techniques associated with queuing and waiting are as follows:
  - **Communication.** Members of a waiting/ queuing crowd must be regularly updated on progress. "Convergers" arriving at the back of the queue should be given a realistic appraisal of the chances of success and the waiting time involved.
  - *Anticipation.* The security forces must be alert to individuals in a queue who become agitated and move quickly to seek an explanation. It may be that there is a genuine grievance that can be addressed. Community representatives and appointed marshals from within that community should be instrumental in any rectifying action, particularly if the issue causing concern is contentious.
  - *Routing.* The route of the queue and the use of lightweight barriers will provide those in the queue with a perception of progress. A winding queue pattern, as used in most airports, will reduce the perception of distance to the filter point, and will give the perception of increased progress.

- **Exploitation.** People waiting in a crowd may present a captive audience for the distribution of information operations literature.

Good-humored interaction by individuals moving amongst members of the crowd can also decrease tension.

– *Negotiation.* Commanders must be prepared to negotiate with identified community representatives. The commencement of crowd violence should not bring negotiation to a halt. Negotiation is best conducted on a one-to-one basis and commanders should not negotiate with a group of people. Cultural issues will dictate the approach to be taken, but adherence to some key principles has proved to work:

   ▪ *Appearance.* Eye contact is vital for successful negotiation. *Key: Commanders should NEVER negotiate wearing sunglasses or other headgear that hide the face and eyes.* Negotiators should adopt as soft a posture as possible and wear the minimum of protective equipment as the threat allows during negotiations.

   ▪ *De-escalatory.* The aim of robust negotiation is to de-escalate the situation and keep or restore peace. Negotiations must therefore be de-escalatory in nature. Commanders must continue to stress their objective as a 'peacemaker' and stress that progress cannot be made until peace is restored. This should be portrayed as a 'common goal' for both parties. Authority should not be negotiated. Concessions may be made as part of the negotiation process but commanders must be clear on what can be conceded and what can not. The right of the security forces to be present and engaged in public order operations should not be negotiated.

   ▪ *Remain Polite, Calm and Firm*—Commanders must remain professional and reasonable throughout negotiations. They must listen to the grievances of the community and attempt to find a solution that de-escalates the situation in accordance with the commander's intent and without compromising the position of the security forces. Negotiations can often be frustrating and commanders must remain calm and focused. Commanders should not make promises but can give assurances that particular grievances will receive appropriate attention.

   ▪ *Clarity*—Commanders should make clear what they want the crowd to do, in particular stipulating the boundaries and limits for forward movement of the crowd. Commanders should make clear the consequences and security force responses to co-operation and non-compliance with security force requests. Commanders should avoid pleading with community representatives and issue deliberate, direct warnings of impending retaliatory action to community representatives in situations where unacceptable crowd behavior exists.

- *Relevance*—The local commander can only influence the immediate and local situation. Local commanders should not engage in discussions about operational and strategic issues and associated grievances as they can lead to inappropriate expressions of empathy by security forces.

- *Retain the Initiative*—Commanders may find themselves taking tactical risks in order to de-escalate a situation and retain the initiative. Junior Commanders must understand what actions they can take on their own initiative. Public disorder situations change rapidly and commanders must remain flexible in order to adapt their plan to changes in crowd behavior. Commanders who stick to a plan regardless of the changes in situation are inviting failure.

- *Equipment considerations include:*
  - *Fire Extinguishers*—Foam and CO_2 extinguishers are the only types acceptable PO operations. Water & dry powder extinguishers must not be used; water causes petrol to spread and dry powder has a very limited effect against petrol.
  - *Ballistic Blankets*—The ballistic blanket is used to protect troops against unexploded ordnance, e.g. pipe-bomb. The blanket must be marked with cyalumes at night so troops know its location.
  - *Loud Speaker*—A loud speaker should be carried by the PO commander and used to give warnings to the crowd.

Security Operations with Indigenous Security Forces

Indigenous security forces are the key to the long-term success of security operations. The same principles that apply when working with indigenous people apply with the security forces. You must understand their needs and develop the force to fit their environment. In the end, they will look more like the insurgents than a U.S. Military unit. There are three basic ways of working with indigenous forces. The first and most basic is partnering, the second is training and the third is advising. Each form requires approval from higher and should be well planned prior to conducting the effort. This section offers a brief overview on the subject; to reference specific guidance and techniques refer to the Marine Corps Foreign Military Training Unit (FMTU) or the U.S. Army Special Forces (SF).

Considerations—The following are basic considerations to aid you in beginning your planning.

- *Use the right people*—Some individuals are better prepared to conduct this type of operation than others. The people should work well off of intent, be masters of their basic skills and be excellent in adapting to fluid situations. Maturity is an absolute requirement.

- *Make them the best force they need to be*—Do not try to make them look like you. They are their own force designed around their own culture and with the proper support may be more suited for dealing with their security environment than you.

  - *Intelligence*—Working with indigenous forces is an excellent way to gather human intelligence. Have a debriefing and reporting plan in place.
  - *Buddy teams*—No U.S. Marine or Soldier should be alone without at least one U.S. buddy. In addition, Guardian Angel applies.
  - *Interpreters*—There must be a substantial interpreter to Marine / Soldier ratio. Ideally, interpreters should be assigned to the each platoon.
  - *Communications*—If you cannot speak with indigenous units then you cannot coordinate.
  - *Safe-House*—When embedded, an advisor team area should be maintained if possible. This aids in the security of classified material and force protection, and it gives advisors a place to *decompress* and discuss issues.
  - *Unity of Command*—As an executive officer does not speak of his discontent with platoon commanders, no advisor should express discontent with other advisors. Discussions stop in the safe-house; after that it is all execution.

- *Positive Attitude*—As with COIN itself, advising, training and partnering with indigenous forces will have achievements and setbacks. You must maintain a positive attitude and not allow your partners to be discouraged by setbacks. Keeping your fighting faith strong amidst frustration is critical.

- *Indigenous forces command indigenous forces*—In some cultures they will be insulted if you attempt to take command, others may allow it to happen but blame short falls on you. Do not get caught in this trap, you are there to either support, advise or train them - nothing else.

- *Build relationships!!!*

- *Build their confidence in you and in themselves*—As soon as possible, put the host nation unit in a live operation. Begin with a simple operation with as little chance of decisive contact as possible and use this as a confidence builder - it will serve the purpose of building their confidence in themselves as well as in you. Small, progressive steps will lead to more success than a large operation that may result in failure. Hold the examples from Chesty Puller and Smedley Butler's as touchstones.

- *Advertise success and explain shortfalls*—As in all COIN operations, the information campaign is paramount—do not lose this initiative.

Partnering—Partnering is the simplest form of working with indigenous forces. This requires joint patrols and planning in support of the host nation forces; fire teams, squads and platoons are used as whole units in direct support of the host nation providing additional combat power.

Training—Training host nation forces normally refers to formalized instruction in a relatively safe area. The training provided should be tailored to the force being trained; their needs and desires are what must be tailored to. Keep in mind that you are not preparing them to be U.S. Marines or Soldiers; you are better equipping them to deal with the issues at hand with the force they already have.

Advising—Advising requires embedded teams attached to a single indigenous unit. Advisors should be chosen for their maturity, MOS proficiency and their ability to succeed in ambiguous situations. Advisors are not in command of the units they are attached to; instead they develop in-depth relationships with the unit based off trust and respect in the advisors' abilities. Individuals placed in advisory roles will have to eat, sleep and fight as part of that host nation unit; they will face a litany of difficult decisions and circumstances. It is imperative to the success of their mission that in every circumstance their actions are just and effective.

ANNEX A:

Patrol Search

1. Types. Details on the conduct of each are provided in this Annex. The types of PS are:

    a.   Personnel search

    b.   Vehicle search

    c.   Route and Vulnerable Point (VP) Checks

    d.   Area (Rummage) search

2. Planning Considerations. The following factors should be considered when planning PS activity:

    a.   Anticipate hostile action. Know how the enemy operates (TTP, etc.) and consider the reaction of the local populace to your activity.

    b.   Isolate the target area, which may involve emplacing a cordon.

    c.   Minimize risk.

    d.   Maintain records. Patrol Search Records (PSR) <u>must</u> be used and, at a minimum, collected by the Unit Search Advisor to assist in the G2 function.

    e.   Electronic Counter Measures (ECM). Ensure that the correct ECM to counter the known threat is employed. Know the constraints of the equipment and plan its use to provide greatest effect. Details on the employment of ECM are given in Ch 8.

    f.   Urban operations. Additional information on planning search in urban environments is given in this section.

3. Equipment. The suggested minimum equipment for a 4-man patrol is given at the end of this Annex.

4. Forensic Awareness

    a. **General.** The aftermath of any incident provides a mass of evidence useful to a forensic scientist to recreate a scene and identify who was involved. This may provide vital intelligence and may help to secure convictions. Such evidence varies in its nature from microscopic fibers to a complete vehicle and much can be destroyed or dislodged if care is not taken to preserve it.

    b. **Evidence preservation.** Forensic evidence may be scattered over a wide area and may not be immediately obvious. Preservation

81

should be on as wide a scale as possible with the following points being adhered to:

(1) Use evidence protection kits: gloves, find bags, find labels. **Do not touch anything** or enter the scene (except to save a life). Do not permit anyone to enter except those qualified to do so (e.g. EOD teams).

(2) Cordon off and preserve the scene intact. Ensure witnesses are identified and either held nearby or have their information recorded for subsequent inquiries.

(3) Keep suspects separated and away from the scene.

(4) Avoid cross-contamination. No soldier who has returned fire should be involved in searching or bagging evidence.

(5) A detailed log of the incident including sketch maps, times and movement details must be kept.

c. **Evidence handling (general rules).** On rare occasions, including the following, it may be necessary for a soldier to handle evidence:

(1) When the local tactical situation makes it unrealistic to cordon an area for any length of time (in some areas locals will deliberately seek to destroy and mask forensic evidence, knowing its value to the prosecution system).

(2) When a minor find has been made.

(3) When a person has been found in possession of an illegal item.

(4) When appropriate agencies are unable to attend. The requirements to provide an auditable trail of evidence handling are paramount:

(5) Appoint only one person as the evidence handler. This person must be able to prove that any article subsequently produced as evidence is the same as that found at the scene.

(6) Appoint one person to keep a written record of events. Before any item is disturbed or removed it must be logged, sketched and, if possible, photographed in situ with any arrestee or detainee suspected to be connected with it.

(7) Avoid cross-contamination. A soldier handling evidence at the scene should not come into contact with any suspect arrested, nor should the soldier move to a different scene and risk transporting evidence.

(8) Wear appropriate protective clothing, especially gloves.

d. **Evidence handling (specific rules).** The following actions should be taken to maximize the preservation of physical evidence:

(1) *Firearms*. The weapon state should be recorded (e.g. magazine fitted, rounds chambered, etc.) If trained on the weapon it should be cleared, attempting not to damage fingerprints on the hand grips (in some areas the threat may dictate that weapons are X-rayed prior to handling). Magazines and ejected rounds should be sealed in separate plastic bags and labeled appropriately.

(2) *Pistols*. Pick up carefully with two fingers on the butt. Avoid the trigger area as the weapon may discharge. **Never** insert a pencil, etc. in the barrel to lift the pistol as vital forensic evidence there may be destroyed. Place pistols and any associated rounds/ magazines in separate, marked plastic bags.

(3) *Long-barrelled Weapons*. Once cleared, place weapons and any associated rounds/ magazines in separate, marked plastic bags. The bags must be sufficiently well marked to make it obvious which rounds/ magazines came from which weapon.

(4) *Ammunition*. Loose rounds should be handled by the rim and placed in marked plastic bags. Avoid using metal objects to pick them up as these can destroy evidence.

(5) *Radio Equipment.* Radio equipment should be moved intact and placed in a marked plastic bag. The exact position of the antenna and any frequency settings should be noted and left undisturbed.

(6) *Clothing.* Clothing will contain useful fibers and thus should be disturbed as little as possible. Place clothing into a clean paper or plastic bag which should then be sealed and labeled.

(7) *Other Items.* Miscellaneous items should be picked up carefully by a corner. Touching smooth flat surfaces which may hold fingerprints should be avoided.

e. **Photography.** When possible, take the following (digital) photographs:

(1) Close up of the article (with a scale if possible)

(2) The article in situ in its immediate surroundings.

(3) The article with any suspect thought to be connected with it.

(4) The general surroundings.

5. Search of Persons

a. **Introduction.** In accordance with ROE suitably trained personnel may be allowed to conduct the search of a person when there is reason to suspect the presence of arms, ammunition or military equipment.

b.   **Conduct.** *The search of persons is to be conducted in the following way:*

(1) *Oral Warning.* An oral warning, through an interpreter if necessary, must be issued.

(2) *Personnel.* There must be a minimum of two soldiers present, one to search and one to provide protection to the searcher and act as a witness

(1) *Females and children.* Females and children under 14 are only to be searched by female soldiers. Male soldiers may search any person using a hand held metal detector.

(2) Do not try to humiliate the subject.

(3) Be professional and avoid being over-familiar with or intimidating the subject.

(4) Use the PSR to record the search.

c. **Types of search.** There are two types of searches for persons:

(1) Quick body search (In the public eye).

(2) Detailed body search (Out of the public eye).

d. **Quick Body Search.** The Quick body search is normally carried out:

(1) When dealing with a large number of people and a detailed body search is not warranted.

(2) As a preliminary to a detailed body search in order to check for the presence of a weapon.

(3) As a preliminary to a detailed body search when the immediate requirement is to secure evidential material that could be jettisoned or destroyed before the detailed search.

e. **Procedure.** The search should be conducted in pairs. The observer should provide protection for the searcher and observe both the searcher and the subject. The following points should be observed:

(1) Establish the identity of the subject and determine the ownership of any baggage.

(2) Inform the subject that they are about to be subject to a body search and why.

(3) To avoid being kicked, kneed or head-butted the searcher should not stand directly in front of or behind the subject.

(4) The searcher should not be distracted or intimidated and should avoid eye contact with the subject.

(5) The observer should watch for non-verbal communication (e.g. increased nervousness).

(6) The searcher should avoid crossing the line of fire of the observer.

(7) The subject should stand with legs slightly apart and arms raised 30 degrees sideways. Do not spread eagle the subject against a vehicle or wall as this may provide an opportunity for forensic evidence to be wiped off hands.

(8) Invite the subject to empty all pockets. Items should be placed in a plastic bag in view of the subject and searched if necessary.

(9) The search should be conducted quickly and systematically from head to foot, down one side and up the other covering all parts of the body front and back. Attention should be paid to pockets, waist bands and all external body depressions: chest, groin, closed hands, armpits, small of back, center of back, and between buttocks.

(10) Use a stroking motion to squeeze clothing and feel for objects through clothing – do not pat. Limbs should be searched using both hands with thumbs and index fingers touching.

(11) Equipment, such as hand held metal detectors (e.g. Hoodlum), may be used to help process/ search large numbers of people.

(12) Search all associated baggage.

(13) Confiscate any prohibited items and preserve as evidence.

f. **Detailed Body Search.** A detailed body search is carried out when:

(1) There are reasonable grounds to suspect that the subject is in possession of illegal items.

(2) A high degree of confidence is required that the subject is not carrying illegal items.

g. **Procedure.** A detailed body search should be conducted using the same procedure as the quick body search but with the addition of the following points:

(1) Ideally, the search should be conducted out of the public eye.

(2) If it is necessary to remove clothing, the subject may do so voluntarily (this fact should be recorded). Only the outer coat, jacket and gloves should be removed in the public eye.

(3) The searcher should pay particular attention to: clothing seams, waist bands, belts, collars, lapels, padding, cuffs, shoes, and socks. Medical dressings can only be examined by a medical practitioner if considered necessary.

6. Vehicle Search

a. **Introduction.** Vehicles are searched for two reasons:

(1) To find and deter the movement of terrorist resources.

(2) To protect potential targets from VOIED placed on/in their vehicles.

b. **Types of vehicle search.** Marines may carry out two types of vehicle searches:

(1) **Initial check.** This is the first part of the weeding process and is carried out on all vehicles stopped.

(2) **Primary search.** This is carried out on vehicles selected for a more detailed examination due to intelligence received or due to suspicion aroused during the initial check.

c. **Initial check.** The initial check is normally carried out with the driver and any passengers in the vehicle. The driver may be asked to open the bonnet (hood) and boot (trunk) for a cursory inspection. The initial check should last no longer than one to three minutes per vehicle.

Sequence. The sequence of the check is as follows:

(1) *Commander*.

(a) Commands and controls the search.

(b) Runs a plate check on the vehicle.

(c) Decides if a primary search is required.

(2) *Designated Speaker*. Speaks to the driver and passengers, through an interpreter, to obtain the following information:

(a) The identities of vehicle occupants.

(b) Confirm the ownership of the vehicle (ask mileage, etc.).

(c) Any other specific information required by G2 and covered in the patrol brief.

(3) *Searcher*. The searcher looks for known 'combat indicators' (e.g. new tires on old vehicles, overloading of rear of vehicle and damaged locks) and observes the reactions of the occupants. The following checks are made:

(a) The outside of the vehicle is inspected.

(b) By looking through the windows the inside of the vehicle is inspected.

(c) The underside of the vehicle is inspected.

(d) The engine and boot compartment are both inspected.

(4) *Cover Man*. The cover man:

(a) Provides protection.

(b) Witnesses the operation.

(5) *Documentation.* A report is required if:

 (a) Anything more than a visual check has been made (e.g. an item in the car is moved by the searcher).

 (b) Damage has been caused in the initial check.

 (c) Documents have been examined or removed.

d. **Primary search.** Vehicles subject to a Primary Search may be inspected by the roadside or directed to an adjacent search area. The search should be as thorough as time permits and must be carried out by a practiced procedure by, ideally, a pair of searchers.

Sequence. The sequence for the Primary Search is as follows:

(1) The occupants are asked to get out of the car and are searched.

(2) The searchers, depending on the situation and existing SOPs, remove helmets and weapons and give them to the cover man who provides security.

(3) The vehicle is searched systematically concentrating on the 5 main areas:

 (a) Exterior

 (b) Underside

 (c) Interior

 (d) Luggage compartment

 (e) Engine Compartment

(4) Search techniques for the search of vehicles and coaches follow.

e. **Documentation.** A report must be completed for a Primary Search.

f. **Action on finds.** If the Primary Search reveals illegal items, the following action should be taken:

(1) The team commander is to send a report through the chain of command.

(2) The incident should be managed in accordance with the guidelines in Chapter 5.

(3) Care should be taken to preserve forensic evidence and avoid cross-contamination.

g. **Secondary Search.** If illegal items are found or further suspicion is aroused during the Primary Search the vehicle may be sent for a Secondary Search. This is a more detailed search conducted in a secure area or base location. The way the vehicle is moved will depend upon its location, the nature of the find, resources available and current SOPs.

h. Search of vehicles is described in figures A-1 through A-3.

Fig A-1: Search of Sedans

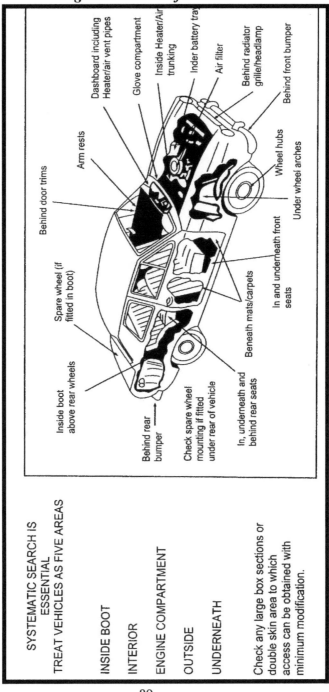

SYSTEMATIC SEARCH IS ESSENTIAL

TREAT VEHICLES AS FIVE AREAS

INSIDE BOOT

INTERIOR

ENGINE COMPARTMENT

OUTSIDE

UNDERNEATH

Check any large box sections or double skin area to which access can be obtained with minimum modification.

Fig A-2: Search of Commercial Vehicles

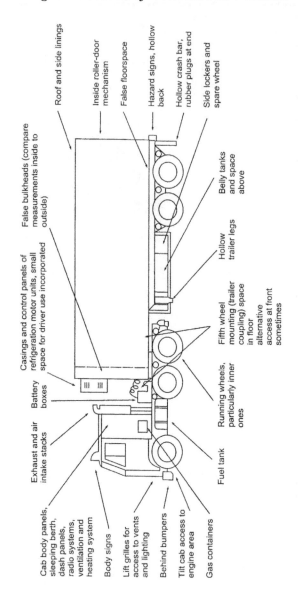

Roof and side linings

Inside roller-door mechanism

False floorspace

Hazard signs, hollow back

Hollow crash bar, rubber plugs at end

Side lockers and spare wheel

False bulkheads (compare measurements inside to outside)

Casings and control panels of refrigeration motor units, small space for driver use incorporated

Battery boxes

Exhaust and air intake stacks

Cab body panels, sleeping berth, dash panels, radio systems, ventilation and heating system

Body signs

Lift grilles for access to vents and lighting

Behind bumpers

Tilt cab access to engine area

Gas containers

Fuel tank

Running wheels, particularly inner ones

Fifth wheel mounting (trailer coupling) space in floor alternative access at front sometimes

Hollow trailer legs

Belly tanks and space above

90

Fig A-3: Search of Buses

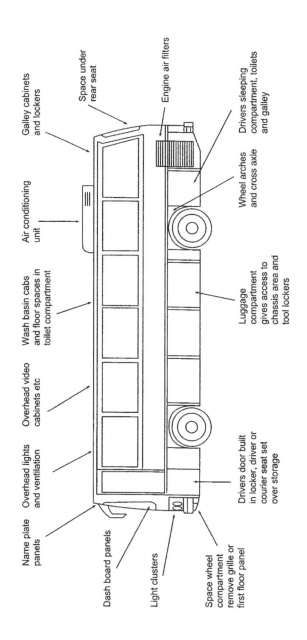

Galley cabinets and lockers

Space under rear seat

Engine air filters

Drivers sleeping compartment, toilets and galley

Air conditioning unit

Wheel arches and cross axle

Wash basin cabs and floor spaces in toilet compartment

Overhead video cabinets etc

Luggage compartment gives access to chassis area and tool lockers

Overhead lights and ventilation

Name plate panels

Drivers door built in locker, driver or courier seat set over storage

Dash board panels

Light clusters

Space wheel compartment remove grille or first floor panel

91

7. **Route and Vulnerable Point Checks**

a. **Introduction.** Routes provide obvious locations for attacks on security forces. Route and VP checks are conducted to ensure that routes are safe to use. Situational awareness is critical and patrols must be thoroughly briefed on the threat, specific enemy TTPs and likely attack locations, etc. before deploying.

b. **Vulnerable Points (VPs).** VPs are likely areas of attack along a given route. Such places include:

(1) Junctions

(2) Culverts

(3) Areas with buildings and walls near the route

(4) Areas with parked or abandoned vehicles near the route

(5) Areas with piles of debris or earth embankments near the route

c. **Methods of Attack.** The enemy is technically sophisticated and has a range of means for conducting attacks at his disposal. These will be refined to incorporate new technology and to counter our own TTPs. Methods of attack are generally in the form of Improvised Explosive Devices (IED) and include blast bombs, mines (hidden in roadside debris, buildings, culverts, etc.) and off-route devices. These may be initiated by a number of ways including:

(1) Command Wires

(2) Radio Control

(3) A combination of radio control and command wire initiation

(4) Victim Operated

(5) Anti-vehicle or Anti-personnel mines

d. **Route and VP Checks.** Route checks can be carried out by vehicle mounted or foot patrols and are normally incorporated into the overall patrol program. The check is performed by three teams of four men and commanded by a patrol commander. Two teams operate on the flanks and the third on the road (the patrol commander is usually located with this team). Electronic Counter Measures (ECM) equipment is likely to be carried to counter current threats. A minimum spacing of 10m between team members should be maintained. The make up and roles of the teams are given below:

(1)   *Flanking Teams.* The flanking teams are identical. They provide protection, check for command wires, scan the route (using binoculars) to identify possible devices (particularly passive infra red (PIR) initiation devices) and look for VPs and firing points. The team will carry ECM. Depending on the

terrain the teams will operate 50 – 75m away from the route. Team deployments are shown in figure A-4.

(2) *Road Team.* The road team consists of two 'hedgerow' men and two road men. The hedgerow men work on opposite sides of the route clearing 1-5m from the edge of the route (where a PIR threat exists the area should be extended to include the outside of any embankments or rubbish out to around 15m). They should scan the opposite side of the road for signs of devices, markers and means of initiation and then check ditches, bunds, piles of rubbish, etc. on their own side. The road men follow behind and are responsible for checking their side of the road and the verge up to the edge of the area searched by the hedgeman. The road team will carry ECM. Arms Explosive Search (AES) dogs are not to be used as part of the road team where a PIR initiation threat exists.

e. **Procedure.** The procedure, shown in figure A-4, is as follows:

(1) *Start Point.* A start point on the road is identified. It should be at least 50m away from any VP. If teams are on foot the start point should be approached across country, not from along the route.

(2) *Flanking Teams.* The Flanking Teams work in a series of bounds. From the start point they move away from the road at a right angle to a distance of 50-75m. They then move roughly parallel to the road, conducting checks for a bound of 80-200m. At the end of each bound a cross-over is made.

(3) *Cross-overs.* These procedures are carried out at the end of each bound in order to detect cables running close to and parallel to the road. The first cross over is usually made after the minimum bound distance of 80m. The drill is as follows:

(a) The Flanking Teams stop opposite each other approximately 50m from the route.

(b) One team, continuing its checks, crosses the route, placing pin markers 1m and 5m from each side of it.

(c) The team then circles the other, static team and returns to its start point, re-crossing the route at the same point. It is critical that the team commander ensures that the wire detector men in the flanking teams cross paths.

(d) Once the team has returned to its original location the next bound can start.

(4) *VPs.* Before being searched by the Road Team a VP must be isolated by the flanking teams conducting cross-overs before and

93

after it as far as possible. Cross-overs should not be made within 50m of a VP. Once isolated one of the Flanking Team commanders may conduct a visual check of the VP with binoculars before continuing on the next bound. The road team, as described below, will conduct the search of the VP.

(5) *Road Team.* The Road Team works a minimum of one bound behind the Flanking Teams and should never approach within 20m of a cross-over point until the following cross-over has been completed. While the Flanking Teams complete their first bound the Road Team checks the start point out to a radius of 20m. The Road Team then:

(a) Checks the route, verges, ditches, bunds, etc.

(b) Checks all VPs by isolating out to a 20m radius (wire detector man plus one) and then searching the VP.

(c) Recovers all markers left by the Flanking Teams.

f. **Single Team VP Checks.** A four man team can be used to check VPs without checking the whole route. The threat should be considered when determining if the team is able to move along the route or should move parallel to the route and approach each VP from a flank. The procedure, shown in figure A-5, is as follows:

(1) *Isolation of the VP.*

(a) The team circles the VP at a radius of 50m checking for command wires, possible devices and firing points.

(b) A 10m spacing must be maintained.

(c) Pin markers are to be placed when crossing the route as for a normal cross-over drill.

(d) The wire detector man must cross his own path.

(e) The team commander should conduct a visual check of the VP during the isolation.

(2) *Search of the VP.* Once isolation is complete the team reforms as a Road Team. It then searches the route between the markers and conducts the VP check as described previously.

g. **Immediate Actions.** In the event that a route or VP check reveals a suspected IED / command wire, the following action should be taken:

(1) By the patrol commander:

(a) Stop all teams, assess the situation and issue orders to relocate teams to a safe location.

(b) Send a report

(c) Establish an ICP and begin incident management procedures (see Chapter 5).

(2) By the man finding or spotting the item:

    (a) Use a mine marker cone to record the location from which the device or item was spotted. This should be no closer than 1m to the object. Do not approach the object once it has been spotted.

    (b) Retrace steps and double-mark a 20m safe lane[1].

    (c) Continue to retrace steps to the last cross-over point and single-mark the route used.

---

[1] As long as the situation permits this route must be clearly marked to permit safe access by specialist resources such as EOD operators. Failure to carry out this drill will require new routes to be cleared to any devices and increase the time taken for follow on operations considerably. No other attempts to clear routes to the device should be made by the patrol.

Fig A-4

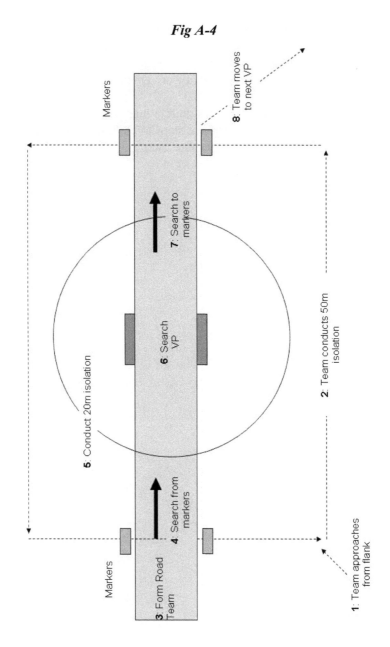

Markers

8: Team moves to next VP

7: Search to markers

6: Search VP

2: Team conducts 50m isolation

5: Conduct 20m isolation

4: Search from markers

3: Form Road Team

Markers

1: Team approaches from flank

96

Fig A-5

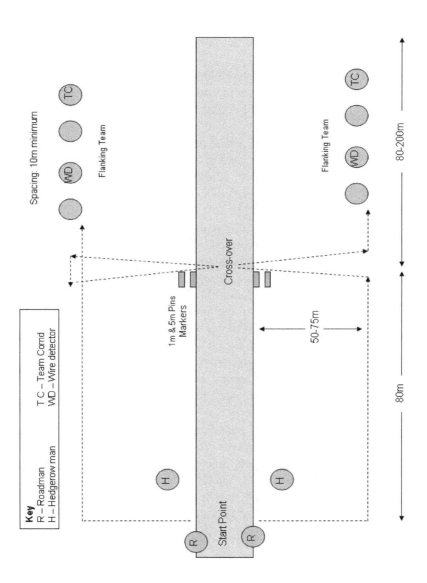

8. Area (Rummage) Search

b. **Introduction.** Terrorist organizations use a system of hides to store and move munitions and weapons. A Rummage Search is an offensive tactic used to deprive the enemy of resources, gain intelligence and provide evidence for prosecution. Hides are categorized as follows:

(1) *Long Term*. These are likely to be well-cited, waterproof constructions that are used for long term storage of resources.

(2) *Transit*. Transit hides are usually built for a specific operation and provide storage en route to a target location. They are normally conveniently marked and cited for an activist to find.

(3) *Short Term*. These are located close to the scene of an incident and are used to conceal equipment immediately before and after an attack, enabling the attacker to leave the contact area 'clean'. These are vulnerable to Rummage.

(a) Hides need to be:
<u>1.</u> Accessible and easily located by night
<u>2.</u> Concealed
<u>3.</u> Available for immediate use
<u>4.</u> Non-attributable

b. **Winthrop Theory.** Winthrop Theory uses the basic requirements of hides and, in particular, the need for reference points to identify possible hide locations. Once a search area has been identified, viewing the ground from the enemy's viewpoint, selecting likely reference points and associated potential hide sites all help to focus the efforts of the search teams. Typical reference points include:

(1) Telegraph poles, gates, barriers and pylons
(2) Trees and bushes
(3) Ends, corners or gaps in fences, walls and hedges
(4) Road signs and street furniture
(5) Distinctive objects such as large rocks or abandoned cars, etc.

c. **Hide Locations.** Hides can be located virtually anywhere – the imagination of the enemy will be the only limit. Examples of areas where hides have been located are given in the table below:

Rural	Urban
Field boundaries and Fields	Waste ground
Roadsides	Derelicts and unoccupied buildings
Woods Copses Plantations	Pavements Roads Gardens
Walls	Sewers Drains
Ditches Culverts	Building sites
Rubbish tips	Graves

d. **Procedure**

The Rummage is conducted in 6 phases:

(1) Phase 1. Over watch, security and deception teams take up position.

(2) Phase 2. Search teams take up position close to the target, select a primary marker and identify likely secondary markers.

(3) Phase 3. Teams carry out standard 20m checks of the area to be rummaged (as a defensive measure). The Primary marker is then occupied.

(4) Phase 4. Primary and secondary markers are confirmed.

(5) Phase 5. Rummage Search of primary and secondary markers is conducted (including 5m checks).

(6) Phase 6. Withdrawal on completion of search.

9. Urban Search Procedures

a. **Introduction.** The very nature of the urban environment dictates that teams and multiple commanders must be prepared to operate with a great deal of flexibility when tasked with carrying out searches.

b. **Aim.** The aim of this section is to provide a planning guide for commanders employed in search ops in the urban environment. It is not intended to be a comprehensive document on urban search procedures.

c. **Threat Assessment.** The threat assessment is critical. Search teams must be familiar with the enemy TTPs. An appreciation of the current situation is essential before planning can start. Once the threat assessment is complete search efforts can be targeted at the most likely sites. The following factors should be considered:

(1) The terrorist method of operation:

(a) Attacks on vehicle patrols

(b) Attacks on foot patrols

(c) Attacks on cordon positions

(d) Disruption of normal life

(2) The type of device and means of initiation likely to be used:

(a) Command Wire IED (CWIED)

(b) Remote Control IED (RCIED)

(c) Victim Operated IED (VOIED)

(d) Timed IED (TIED)

(3) Likely locations of a device:

(a) Road junctions

(b) Choke points - alleyways, cul-de-sacs, etc.

(c) Patrol routes. Honesty traces should be checked to avoid   pattern setting.

(d) Obvious ICP locations and cordon positions

d. **Incident management.** The following principles apply to any incident:

(1) *Confirm* the find (record a description, its location and produce a sketch).

(2) *Clear* the area (100m for a briefcase size device, 200m for a car and 400m for a large vehicle – keep out of line of sight).

(3) *Cordon* the area. Remember 5 and 20m checks!

(4) *Control* the cordon (including the movement of specialist assets).

(5) Check for secondary hazards (such as fuel storage facilities).

10. Patrol Equipment. The suggested minimum search equipment for a 4-man patrol is as follows:

Ser	Item	Qty	Remarks
(a)	(b)	(c)	(d)
1	Search documentation	5	PSR
2	Hand held metal detector	2	
3	Digging tool	1/ man	Trowel
4	Shovel	1	
5	Patrol wire detector	1	
6	Working gloves	4 pairs	
7	Notebook & pencil	1/ man	Patrol notebook
8	Mine tape	20m/man	
9	Camera	1	Digital
10	Evidence bag	1/ man	Evidence collection / preservation
11	Latex gloves	1/ man	As 10(d)
12	Evidence awareness kits	1/ man	As issued in theatre
13	Search bag	1/ man	
14	Pin markers	20/ man	
15	Mine marker cone	2 / man	

Basic Observation Skills

1. **Aim.** The aim of this chapter is to define the basic observation skills that need to be acquired by all soldiers and discuss how they are applied to gain and improve Situational Awareness.

2. **General.** To exhibit effective Situational Awareness you must be able combine a background understanding of the environment, the indigenous population and how they all interact with up-to-date knowledge of the threat that you are facing, what friendly and neutral forces are doing around you and how their activities may affect your situation. Above all, you must pay attention to your surroundings. Effective Situational Awareness is all about being proactive. You must be able to identify potential threats and dangers in advance and ignore distractions (anything which takes your focus off the job at hand). To achieve all this together is not difficult if the approach is rigorous, focused and you have had the correct background briefings and have undergone appropriate training.

3. **Danger Areas/Situations.** It is important to understand that there are areas and situations which will pose a greater threat than others. It is necessary to be at a state of alert directly proportional to that threat. Identifying danger in advance will give you the opportunity to prepare yourself accordingly but in order to be able to reduce your level of alert when appropriate you must be aware of the bigger picture. Keep in mind that the threat will change and though an area may be safe for a period of time, it may not always be so.

4. **Pre-incident Indicators.** Pre-incident Indicators are subtle clues that something is not right. Anything that is unusual or out of place requires a closer look. Use your instincts: you may be suspicious, afraid or apprehensive about something. While these feelings cannot be allowed to affect the mission they may, if used prudently, lead to a successful outcome. It is better to be cautious than careless. Avoid thinking about the past; focus on the present. Doing so will allow you to pick up on subtle clues with greater ease and success.

5. **Action.** Once you have discovered something out of the ordinary you should consider what you are going to do with the information you have

gathered (i.e. look for escape routes, cover, concealment). At this point, it is vital that your reaction is appropriate and timely and that you do not, in the process of taking that action, forget what triggered it in the first place.

6. **Training and Briefing.** Only through consistent and thorough application of skills and tools (training), coupled with a comprehensive understanding of the environment and threat (briefing), can you create appropriate levels of situational awareness to cope in a complex military environment.[1] In a military context SA can be defined as:

> *"An individual's understanding of the operational environment including friendly and enemy forces and their intent, the physical environment and other factors in the context of his role and mission."[2]*

7. **Command.** *Understand.* Commanders at all levels must ensure that their soldiers possess a full understanding of who (including local "personalities") and what they will be up against and the environment in which they will be operating. This will involve engendering:

a. *Cultural Awareness.* All soldiers must be aware of differences in the cultures of the enemy, and of the indigenous population and (to a lesser extent) of coalition partners. This will enable the soldier to understand their behavior patterns and what to expect in different situations. He will thus be better able to anticipate the enemy's actions and will be able to communicate more effectively where the situation demands.

b. *Environmental Awareness.* Commanders and soldiers must be fully aware of the terrain and weather in theatre and must be fully prepared (trained and equipped) to operate effectively once deployed.

c. *Threat Awareness.* The threat must be understood by all. Commanders at all levels must ensure that their soldiers are completely aware of the enemy's capabilities and how and when he is likely to employ them. Detailed knowledge of the threat, maintained vigilance and an understanding of the Combat Indicators will enhance the chance of preventing a successful enemy attack (e.g.

---

[1] UK Army Field Manual Vol 1 Pt 1 Formation Tactics.
[2] UK Army Field Manual Vol 1 Pt 8 Command and Staff Procedures.

Guidance on Suicide Bombers[3]). The threat is limited only by the imagination and technical capability of the enemy. Any list of possible threats will therefore not be comprehensive. Such a list is provided at the end of this Annex.

d. ***Combat Indicators.*** Units and soldiers able to establish detailed knowledge of the "pattern of life" in their AO are at an advantage as there are often tell-tale signs that an incident is about to take place. These may be spotted by alert soldiers:

(1) During the terrorists' preliminary reconnaissance

(2) While terrorists set up an incident

(3) In the period immediately prior to its initiation

(4) Examples of Combat Indicators are shown in figure B-1. Even if patrolling in an unfamiliar environment, these combat indicators can be recognized as:

---

[3] UK Army Field Manual Vol 1 Pt 11 BG Tactics.

The Absence Of The Normal Or The Presence Of The Abnormal		
Absence Of The Normal	Presence Of The Abnormal	Implications
	Tracking of patrols Tracking by known terrorists from likely firing positions	Terrorists need exact information as to a patrol's location, strength, disposition and attitude before they will engage it. Are trackers providing the final confirmation for an attack should proceed? Do they show apprehension, tension and excitement or just indifference?
Women, children and other passers-by suddenly vacate a street or are absent from a normally busy area	An aggressive crowd suddenly disappears	Clearing the way for a shoot or detonation of a device and avoiding collateral damage?
	Curtains either open or drawn at the "wrong" time of day	Another sign of a house takeover or simply a signal that your patrol is in the area. Does interior light flood out to illuminate a soldier passing by the window?
	Known terrorists making themselves obviously seen on foot or in vehicles	A distraction?
Routine traffic fails to show or is late. Lack of cars on a normally busy road	Cars or vans unusually low on the suspension	Have they been hijacked for use as proxy bombs or mortar baseplates? Have locals been warned to avoid an attack zone?
	Footprints, disturbed vegetation at potential ambush sites	May indicate presence of potential attackers at FP or CP
	Recent digging. Sudden flocking of birds	Dug-in CW or device? Rural activity may indicate presence of potential attackers

	Posts, flags, bags, cones or other conspicuous objects placed at the roadside or above head-height	Potential markers for command wire IED, IAAG, PRIG, horizontal mortar or similar attacks, especially against mobile patrols

Figure B-1: Examples of Combat Indicators

e. **Actions.** Too often soldiers will have seen evidence of an attack unfolding but fail to act on the information. It is imperative that all combat indicators are:

(1) **Recorded.** If you are not the immediate target someone else may be at present or in the near future. Record all details in the Patrol Report.

(2) **Reported.** Have the confidence to voice your concerns to the team/patrol commander and Ops Room. Make sure everyone is alerted and you may prevent the attack by your change of profile.

(3) **Acted on.** If you react as if you have seen something, you may actually startle the terrorist into exposing his position and subsequently you will gain the initiative. Do not continue with your original patrol plan; the "enemy" factor has changed – so must your estimation of the threat.

f. **Terrorist SOPs.** Terrorist attacks seldom follow identical patterns, however if an attack has been successful it is likely to be repeated if the opportunity presents itself. For this reason information must be disseminated ASAP. A terrorist attack will normally follow a certain sequence of events which may be as illustrated at the end of this Annex.

8. **Surveillance.** Surveillance describes the operational tasks of protective overwatch and information gathering. It provides the ability to defeat terrorism through proactive operations based on a good intelligence picture with real time imagery allowing the military to disrupt terrorist operations. Surveillance may be considered a refinement of basic reconnaissance but while training is required to conduct observation effectively, overt surveillance is simply a matter of following basic procedures. Surveillance is assisted by state-of-the-art optical equipment, radar, thermal and infra-red imaging (TI and II) devices but still relies on close observation, logging and reporting activity. Covert

surveillance tends to focus on the monitoring of a specific target (person or place) based on current threat. Overt surveillance observes a specific area within visual range of the OP, known as its footprint, providing protection, deterrence and information on terrorist and terrorist related activity.

9. **Surveillance Skills.** Surveillance has become a specialized operation but it is one that any soldier may be required to undertake, for example, while observing from a security outpost. Soldiers are often rotated through operational cycles to keep interest and motivation high but the surveillance skills must be maintained at a high level by practicing individual and collective skills whenever possible. The skills required for conducting surveillance from an outpost, OP or monitoring suite are numerous. They can be primarily broken down into:

    a.   Observing, logging and reporting skills

    b.   Communications and administration

    c.   Equipment familiarity

10. **Core Skills.** Core individual observing skills, which must be taught before deployment and practiced regularly, are:

A – H (Describing Persons)	SCRIM (Describing Vehicles)
A – Age	S – Shape
B – Build	C – Color
C – Clothes	R – Registration
D – Distinguishing marks	I – Identifying features
E – Elevation (Height)	M – Make/ Model
F – Face	
G – Gait	
H – Hair	

11. **Continuity of Evidence.** One of the primary roles of overt surveillance is to provide detailed information for others to use in their attempts to cause attrition. This information could also potentially be used as evidence in a court of law to secure convictions. Soldiers must therefore be "evidence aware" to ensure that opportunities from which convictions could arise are not missed because of errors in evidence continuity or information handling.

106

12. **Preservation of Forensic Evidence.** Evidence awareness extends to the preservation of evidence at the scene of an incident. It is recognized that complete and effective preservation of forensic evidence is a skill that requires a significant amount of training and scientific equipment. Under most circumstances it will therefore be necessary to involve police however; there will be times when this is impracticable due to the security situation. When this is the case it will be necessary for the patrol leader or incident commander to ensure that the scene is appropriately photographed and relevant evidence is "bagged and tagged" with as little contamination as possible.

The Threat

1. All Marines/Soldiers are encouraged to "**think terrorist**" and attempt to undermine his opportunities by presenting a difficult target.

THREAT WEAPON	CHARACTERISTICS	RANGE	DEPLOYMENT	EFFECT
Petrol Bomb	Bottle filled with petrol, possibly mixed with paint, acid, etc. Wick protrudes from neck. Lit immediately before throwing	15–20 m	Mostly during minor aggro or riot using crowd as cover. Thrower may expose himself to view	Normally can be avoided but potentially lethal if thrown at close range against unprotected skin
Grenades				
RDG-5	Commercial anti-personnel fragmentation grenade	15–20m	As above	Shrapnel effect increases with confined space
Mk 15 "Coffee Jar"	Commercial explosive and detonator, initiates on glass shattering and releasing spring	10–15m	As above plus dropped from high points, bridges, flats, etc.	Considerable anti-personnel effect, limited anti-vehicle effect

THREAT WEAPON	CHARACTERISTICS	RANGE	DEPLOYMENT	EFFECT
IAAG	Shaped charge, "drogue" bomb. Destroyed on impact	5–10m	As above, thrower may expose himself to view if used horizontally	Modern vehicle armour lessens impact
Shoot Close Quarters Action	Handgun, shotgun or rifle used at close range	0–2m	Victim is shot at close range, usually several times	Usually fatal
"Cowboy"	Random, unplanned shoot and run, using high or low velocity weapon	15–50m	Usually used to "blood" young terrorist. Lacks determination, escape uppermost intent	Difficult to achieve a significant hit
Automatic multi-weapon	Well-planned attack from prepared firing positions with mutually supporting mix of AK47, Mortars, HMG, etc.	20–300m	Determined ASU, especially in rural setting, with vehicular escape arranged	Can destroy lightly armoured vehicles and troops in the open
Snipe	Single, well-aimed shot from HV weapon, including commercial sniper rifles with optic sights such as Barrett .50	30–100+m	Zeroed weapon used by dedicated terrorist with good tracking and escape systems in place	Usually fatal
Shoulder-launched devices PRIG	Home-made equivalent of RPG. Loud signature. Disposable launcher	5–30m	Usually fired in enfilade from prepared FP offering cover from view	Will damage armoured vehicles
RPG 7/RPG 22	Commercial light anti-armour weapons. RPG 7 re-loadable, RPG 22 disposable tube			Will defeat armour

THREAT WEAPON	CHARACTERISTICS	RANGE	DEPLOYMENT	EFFECT
Horizontal Mortar Mk 12 or Mk 16		0–250m	Urban from vehicle, rural dug in to bank	Will defeat armour
Explosion CWIED	Various-sized explosive pack housed in metal or plastic container (milk churn, fertilizer bag, plastic barrel), usually home-made mix with commercial booster and detonator, initiated by command wire which may be dug-in	5–700m (7m shortest urban CW)	Urban CW tends to be shorter and may be surface laid at short notice. Rural can be longer and spit-locked into ground a considerable distance. Targets are predicted and tracked – markers may be used to confirm target in killing zone	Considerable collateral damage over a widespread area. Depending on the amount of explosive used and direction of blast it may defeat armoured vehicles.
RCIED	As above, except device initiated by remote means, whether light, laser, radio, telephone or other	15–300m	Certain types can be inhibited therefore terrorist looks to exploit slack drills.	As above
VOIED	As above, except device initiated by pressure pad, trip-wire, light-sensitive switch, mercury tilt switch or similar	Immediate area	Terrorist need not remain in situ once device primed. Favored at derelicts, attractive items, predicted harbor areas, under vehicles, etc.	As above

Terrorist SOPs

1. Terrorist attacks seldom follow identical patterns, however if an attack has been successful it is likely to be repeated if the opportunity presents itself. Attacks will normally follow a certain sequence of events.

Event	Remarks
Reconnaissance	The gunman or bomber may well recon the target area and his potential escape routes, looking for markers, good line-of-sight, suitable firing positions and so on
Tracking/ Lookout screen	Confirmatory information on target location, timings and disposition will be provided by a screen of trackers. Trackers will try to identify • unit boundaries • routes used • cover positions and locations adopted • timings • attitude/ alertness • strength and composition Lookouts, including youngsters, will provide a warning system to cover the movement of weapons, approach of the gunman/ bomber, approach of the target and appearance of threats to the escape route (such as an unforeseen patrol). Mobile phones, CB radios and walkie-talkies may be used if a simple hand-signal system cannot cope
Provision of weapons and explosives	The plan will normally be for weapons and explosives to be moved into the attack zone immediately before the incident and removed from the scene immediately afterwards. In urban areas this may be achieved by a supply chain of terrorists; while in rural areas the actual gunman/ bomber may carry the munitions in and out of position himself. Temporary, transit hides may be used both before and after an attack to safeguard the weapons pending re-location to a deep hide

Event	Remarks
Firing Points/ House takeovers	A safe and unsuspected FP for shoots and IED initiation may take the form of a nearby building. If these are occupied, terrorists may take over the house and hold the occupants captive until after the attack. Such FP may be adapted to suit the weapon being used, for example, roof slates, air vents or window glass may be moved to accommodate a long-barrelled weapon. The family car may be stolen for use as an escape vehicle. Neither the house nor the car will attract attention as they are inevitably "untraced"
The attack	Timings, range and method of attack will vary enormously depending on the type of attack, the environment, the caliber of terrorist and even the weather.
Post attack/ escape	The terrorist will wish to distance himself from the scene by escaping on foot, bike or other vehicle. His immediate concern is to ditch clothing which may tie him forensically to the scene. If escape routes are blocked, he may try to blend into the community, possibly by entering other occupied buildings. The terrorist will always want to place some kind of barrier between himself and pursuing SF. Obvious examples are walls and fences, however he may also use inter-unit boundaries, open ground (clear field of fire) or groups of civilians, including children. Inevitably the terrorist will attempt to leave behind an observer to note SF reaction and tactics as well as the result of the attack.

The Twenty-Eight Articles
Fundamentals of Company-level
Counterinsurgency

By David Kilcullen

This paper reflects the author's personal judgments and does not represent the views of any department or agency of the U.S. Government or any other government.

Introduction

Your company has just been warned for deployment on counterinsurgency operations. You have read David Galula, T.E. Lawrence and Robert Thompson. You have studied FM 3-24 and you understand the history, philosophy and theory of counterinsurgency. You watched *Black Hawk Down* and *The Battle of Algiers,* and you know this will be the most difficult challenge of your life.

But time is short: how do you prepare? What does the theory actually mean, at the company level? How do the principles translate once you get into theater – in the dark, with friendly forces shooting at you, the GPS down, the media reporting your every move, the locals complaining in a language you don't understand, and an unseen enemy killing your people by ones and twos? How do you make the doctrine work? Be comforted: you are not the first to feel this way. And though there are no universal answers, there *are* fundamentals you can apply.

What follows are observations from collective experience: the distilled essence of what those who went before you learned. They complement, but do not replace the theory. They are expressed as commandments, for clarity – but of course they are nothing of the sort. Rather, they are more in the nature of folklore. Apply them judiciously and skeptically.

Preparation

Time is short during pre-deployment, but you will never have more time to think than you have now. Now is your chance to prepare yourself and your command. The first nine articles relate to preparation:

1. **Know your patch.** Know the people, the topography, economy, history and culture. Know every village, road, field, population group, tribal leader and ancient grievance. Your task is to become the world expert on your particular district. If you don't know precisely where you will be operating, study the province or the general area. Read the map like a book: study it every night before sleep, and re-draw it from memory every morning, until you understand its patterns intuitively. Develop a mental model of your area – a framework in which to fit every new piece of knowledge you acquire. Study handover notes from predecessors; better still, get in touch with the unit in theater and pick their brains. In an ideal world, intelligence officers and area experts would brief you. This rarely happens: and even if it does, there is no substitute for personal mastery. Share out specific aspects of the operational area among the platoon leaders and non-commissioned officers: have each individual develop a personal specialization and brief the others. Neglect this knowledge, and it will kill you.

2. **Diagnose the problem.** Once you know your area, you can begin to diagnose the problem. Who are the insurgents? What drives them? What makes local leaders tick? Counterinsurgency is fundamentally a competition, between you and the insurgent, as to which side can more effectively mobilize the population in support of its agenda. So you must understand what motivates the people and how to mobilize them. Work this problem collectively with your platoon and squad leaders: discuss it back and forth, explore the problem, understand what you are facing, and seek a consensus. If this sounds un-military, get over it. Once you are in theater, situations will arise too quickly for orders, or even a commander's intent. Your corporals and private soldiers will have to make snap judgments with strategic impact. The only way to help them is to give them a shared understanding, then trust them to think for themselves on the day.

3. **Organize for intelligence.** In counterinsurgency, killing the enemy is easy. Finding him is often nearly impossible. Intelligence and operations have a symbiotic relationship. Your operations will be intelligence driven, but your intelligence will come mostly from your own operations. Intelligence will not be a "product", prepared and served up by higher headquarters. Rather, it will be feedback on your own actions. So you must organize for intelligence. You will need a company S2 or non-commissioned officer, and a company intelligence section – including some analysts. You may need platoon S2s and S3s, and you will need a company reconnaissance and surveillance element. You will also need to select people for human intelligence tasks. You will probably not get augmentation for this: but you must still do it. Choose the smartest soldiers and put them in the S2 section and the R&S squad. You will have one less rifle squad: but the intelligence section will pay for itself in lives and effort saved.

4. **Organize for inter-agency operations.** Almost everything in counterinsurgency is inter-agency. And everything important – from policing to intelligence to civil-military operations to trash collection – will involve your company working with civilian actors and local indigenous partners you can't control, but whose success is essential for yours. Train the company staff in inter-agency operations – get a briefing from the State Department, aid agencies and the local Police or Fire Brigade. Create point-men in each squad who are trained to deal with the inter-agency. Realize that civilians find rifles, helmets and body armor intimidating. Learn how not to scare them. Most importantly, realize that your company's operations may create a temporary breathing space, but long-term development and stabilization by civilian agencies will ultimately win the war.

5. **Travel light and harden your CSS.** You will be weighed down with body armor, rations, extra ammunition, communications gear, and a thousand other things. The enemy will carry a rifle, an extra magazine, a *shemagh* and a water bottle if he is lucky. Unless you ruthlessly lighten your load and enforce a culture of speed and mobility, the insurgents will consistently out-run and out-maneuver you. But in lightening your load, remember to harden your CSS. The enemy will attack your weakest points. Most attacks on coalition forces in Iraq in 2004 and 2005, outside pre-planned combat actions like the two battles of Fallujah or Operation Iron Horse, were against

CSS installations and convoys. You do the math. Ensure your CSS assets are hardened, have communications, and are trained in combat operations. They may do more fighting than your rifle squads.

6. **Find a political officer.** In a force optimized for counterinsurgency, you might receive a political adviser at company level. This could be a civilian diplomat or military foreign area officer, able to speak the language and navigate the intricacies of local politics. Back on planet Earth, the Corps and Division commander will get a POLAD: you will not. So you need to improvise. Find a political adviser from among your own people – perhaps an officer, perhaps not (see article 8). Someone with a background in practical politics and a "feel" for the environment will do better than a political science graduate. Don't try to be your own political adviser: you need to be fully aware of the political dimension at all times, but this is a different task. Also, don't give one of your intelligence people this role. They can help, but their task is to understand the environment – the political officer's job is to help you shape it.

7. **Train the squad leaders – then trust them.** Counterinsurgency is a squad and platoon leader's war, and often a private soldier's war. Battles are won or lost in seconds: whoever can bring combat power to bear in a split-second, on a street corner, will win. The commander on the spot controls the fight. You must train your squad leaders to act intelligently and independently without orders. If your squad leaders are competent, you can get away with average company or platoon staffs. The reverse is not the case. Training should focus on basic skills: marksmanship, patrolling, security on the move and at the halt, basic drills. When in doubt, spend less time training company and platoon drills, and more time training squads. Ruthlessly replace leaders who do not make the grade. But once your people are trained, and you have developed a shared operational "diagnosis", you must trust them. We all talk about this, but few company or platoon leaders really do trust their people. In counterinsurgency, you have no choice.

8. **Rank is nothing: talent is everything.** Not everyone is good at counterinsurgency. Many people don't understand the concept, and some who do can't execute it. It is difficult, and in a conventional force only a few people will master it. Anyone can learn the basics,

but there are a few "naturals". Learn how to spot these people and put them into positions where they can make a difference. Rank matters far less than talent – a few good men led by a smart junior non-commissioned officer can succeed in counterinsurgency, where hundreds of well-armed soldiers under a mediocre senior officer will fail.

9. **Have a game plan.** The final preparation task is to develop a game plan: a mental picture of how you see the operation developing, a time-phased concept of what you intend to achieve. You will be tempted to try and do this too early. But wait: as your knowledge improves, you will get a better idea of what needs to be done, and a clearer idea of your own limitations. Senior commanders might call this "operational design", or "campaign planning". At the company level, you just need a simple robust idea of what to achieve and how. One approach that works is to identify basic phases in your operation: e.g. "establish dominance, build local networks, marginalize the enemy". Make sure you can easily transition between phases, both forward (if you are succeeding) or backward in case of setbacks. Just as the insurgent can adjust his activity to yours, you must have a game plan simple enough to survive setbacks without collapsing. This game plan is the "treatment" concept that matches the shared "diagnosis" your commanders carry around in their heads – it must be simple, and known by everyone.

The Golden Hour

Preparation is over. You have deployed, completed reception and staging, and perhaps (if you are lucky) attended the in-country counterinsurgency school. Now it is time to enter your operational area and start your tour. This is the golden hour. Mistakes made now will haunt you for the rest of the tour, while early successes will set the tone for success. You will look back on your early actions and cringe at your clumsiness. So be it: but you must act.

10. **Be there.** The most fundamental rule of counterinsurgency is *presence*: be there. You can almost never outrun the enemy. If you are not present when an incident happens, there is usually little you can do about it. So your first order of business is to establish presence. If you cannot do this throughout your sector, then do it wherever you can. This demands a residential approach to

117

counterinsurgency – living in your area of responsibility, in close proximity to the population, rather than raiding into the area from remote, secure bases. Movement on foot, sleeping in local villages, night patrolling: all these seem more dangerous than they are. Driving around in an armored convoy – visiting your area for daytrips, like a tourist in hell – degrades situational awareness, makes you a target and is ultimately more dangerous.

11. **Beware of first impressions**. Insurgencies are like the road toll: just because you don't see car wrecks every day does not mean they are not happening. Unless you happen to be on the spot when an incident occurs, you will have only second-hand reports to go on. This fragmentation and "disaggregation" of the battlefield – particularly in urban areas – means that first impressions are often highly misleading in counterinsurgency. Of course, you cannot avoid making your own judgments. But if possible, check them with an older hand or a trusted local. If you can, keep one or two officers from your predecessor unit for the first part of the tour. You will have a natural tendency act on your impressions as soon as you arrive – but try to avoid a rush to judgment.

12. **Prepare for handover from Day One.** Believe it or not, you will not resolve the insurgency on your watch. Your tour will end, and your successors will need your corporate knowledge. Start handover folders, in every platoon and specialist squad, from day one – ideally, you would have inherited these from your predecessors, but if not you must start them. The folders should include lessons learned, details about the population, village and patrol reports, updated maps, photographs – anything that will help newcomers master the environment. Computerized databases are fine, but keep good back-ups and ensure you have hard copy of key artifacts and documents. This is boring, tedious and essential. Over time, you will create a corporate memory that keeps your people alive.

13. **Build trusted networks**. Once you have settled into your sector, your key task is to build trusted networks. This is the true meaning of the phrase "hearts and minds", which comprises two separate components. "Hearts" means persuading people their best interests are served by your success; "Minds" means convincing them that resisting you is pointless. Note that neither of these concepts has anything to do with whether or not people like you. Calculated self-

interest, not emotion, is what counts. Over time, if you successfully build networks of trust, these will grow like roots into the population, displacing the enemy's networks, bringing him out into the open to fight you, and seizing the initiative. These networks include local allies, community leaders, local security forces, NGOs and other friendly or neutral non-state actors in your area, and the media. Start a charm offensive. Conduct village and neighborhood surveys to identify needs in the community – and then follow through to meet them, build common interests, develop leverage and mobilize popular support. This activity is your true main effort: everything else is secondary. Actions that help build trusted networks serve your cause. Actions – even killing high-profile targets – that undermine trust or disrupt your networks help the enemy.

14. **Start easy.** If you were trained in maneuver warfare you know about surfaces and gaps. This applies to counterinsurgency as much as any other form of maneuver. Don't try to crack the hardest nut first – don't go straight for the main insurgent stronghold, or try to provoke a decisive showdown, or focus your efforts on villages where the population supports the insurgents. Instead, start easy. Do this by building extending your influence through the locals' own networks. Go with, not against, the grain of local society: first win the confidence of a few villages, and then see who they trade, intermarry or do business with. Now win these people over. Soon enough you will strike a hard nut and the showdown will come. But now you have local allies, a mobilized population and a trusted network at your back. Do it the other way round and no one will mourn your failure.

15. **Dominate the enemy early.** When you do encounter the enemy in this early phase, your aim is to stamp your dominance into his psyche. Some company commanders have previously sought to get a kill within the first 24 hours of moving into a new area of operations. Others have consciously used a sledgehammer to crack a nut. This can be overly aggressive – and it depends on the enemy being stupid enough to present you with a clear-cut target, a rare windfall in counterinsurgency – but the concept is sound. Like any other form of armed propaganda, dominating the enemy early in the tour sets the tone for what comes later, and helps you seize the initiative – which you have probably lost due to the inevitable hiatus entailed by the handover-takeover with your predecessor unit. Avoiding collateral

damage is critical at this early stage. So seek clear-cut targets, smash them mercilessly if found, but apply stringent rules of engagement.

16. **Practice deterrent patrolling.** Establish patrolling methods that deter the enemy from attacking you. Often our patrolling approach seems designed to provoke, then defeat, enemy attacks. This is counter-productive: it leads to a raiding, day-tripping mindset or, worse, a bunker mentality. Instead, practice deterrent patrolling. There are many methods for this, including "multiple" patrolling where you flood an area with numerous small patrols working together. Each is too small to be a worthwhile target, and the insurgents never know where all the patrols are – making an attack on any one patrol extremely risky. Other methods include so-called "blue-green" patrolling, where you mount daylight overt humanitarian patrols, which go covert at night and hunt specific targets. Again, the aim is to keep the enemy off balance, and the population reassured, through constant and unpredictable patrolling activity – which, over time, deters attacks and creates a more permissive environment. A reasonable rule of thumb is that one to two thirds of your force should be on patrol at any time, day or night.

17. **Be prepared for setbacks.** Setbacks are normal in counterinsurgency, as in every other form of war. You will make mistakes. You will lose people. You may occasionally kill or detain the wrong person. You may fail in building or expanding networks. If this happens, don't lose heart. Simply drop back to the previous phase of your game plan and recover your balance. It is normal in company counterinsurgency operations for some platoons in your sector to be doing well, while others do badly. This is not necessarily evidence of failure. Give local commanders the freedom to adjust their posture to local conditions, in a flexible manner. This creates elasticity that allows you to survive setbacks.

18. **Remember the global audience.** One of the biggest differences between the counterinsurgencies our fathers fought and the ones we face today is the omnipresence of globalized media. Most houses in Iraq have one or more satellite dishes. Web bloggers, print, radio and television reporters and others are monitoring and reporting your every move. When the enemy ambushes your patrols or sets off a car bomb, they do so not because they want to destroy one more track, but because they want graphic images of a burning vehicle and dead

bodies for the evening news. Beware the "scripted enemy", who plays to a global audience and seeks to defeat you in the court of global public opinion. You counter this by training your people to always bear in mind the global audience, assume that everything they say or do will be publicized, and most importantly by befriending the media. Get the press on-side: help them get their story, and trade information with them. Good relationships with non-embedded media – especially local indigenous media - can dramatically increase your situational awareness, and help get your message across to the global and local audience.

19. **Covet your enemy's wife – but keep the children at arm's length**. Most insurgent fighters are men. But in traditional societies, women are hugely influential in forming social networks the insurgents use for support. Winning over neutral or friendly women, through targeted social and economic programs, builds networks of enlightened self-interest that eventually undermine the insurgents. You need your own female counterinsurgents, including inter-agency people, to do this effectively. Win the women, and you own the family unit. Own the family, and you take a big step forward in mobilizing the population. Conversely, though, stop your people fraternizing with local children. Your troops are homesick; they want to drop their guard with the kids. But children are sharp-eyed, lacking in empathy, and willing to commit atrocities their elders would shrink from. The insurgents are watching: they will notice any act of friendship between your people and local children, and will either harm the children in punishment, or use them against you. Similarly, stop your people throwing candies or presents to children. It attracts them to our vehicles, creates crowds the enemy can exploit, and leads to children being run over. Harden your heart and keep the children at arm's length, except through their mothers.

20. **Take stock regularly.** Develop metrics early in the tour. These will need refining as the operation progresses, but should cover a range of social, informational, military and economic issues. Use these intelligently to form an overall impression of progress in your sector – not in a mechanistic "traffic light" fashion. Typical metrics include: percentage of combat engagements initiated by our forces versus those initiated by insurgents; longevity of friendly local leaders in positions of authority; number and quality of tip-offs on insurgent activity that originate spontaneously from the population;

local economic activity at markets and shops. These mean virtually nothing as a snapshot – it is trends over time that help you track progress in your sector.

Groundhog Day

Now you are in "steady state". Your insertion phase is over, you are established in your sector, and your people are settling into that "groundhog day" mentality that hits every unit at some stage during every tour. It will probably take at least the first third of the tour for your people to become effective in the environment, if not longer. Then in the last period you will struggle against the short-timer mentality. So this middle part of the tour is when you do your most productive work – but keeping the flame alive, and bringing the local population along with you, takes immense leadership.

21. **Build a "single narrative".** Since counterinsurgency is a competition to mobilize popular support, it pays to know how people are mobilized. In most societies there are opinion-makers: local leaders, pillars of the community, religious figures, media personalities, and others who set trends and influence public perceptions. This influence – and the pernicious influence of the insurgents – often takes the form of a "single narrative": a simple, unifying, easily-expressed narrative that organizes people's experience and provides a framework for understanding events. Nationalist and ethnic historical myths, or sectarian creeds, provide such a narrative. The Iraqi insurgents have one, as do al-Qa'eda and the Taliban. To undercut their influence you must build you own alternative narrative: or better yet, tap into an existing narrative that excludes the insurgents. For example, you might use a nationalist narrative to marginalize foreign fighters in your area, or a narrative of national redemption to undermine former regime elements that have been terrorizing the population. At the company level, you do this in baby steps, by getting to know local opinion-makers, winning their trust, learning what motivates them and building on this to find a single narrative that emphasizes the inevitability and rightness of your ultimate success. This is art, not science: but it is for tasks like this that you need a good intelligence section, a political officer and close inter-agency relationships.

122

22. **Local forces should mirror the enemy, not ourselves.** By this stage, you will be working closely with local forces, training or supporting them, and building indigenous capability. The natural tendency is to build forces in our own image, with the aim of eventually handing our role over to them. This is a mistake. Instead, local indigenous forces need to mirror the enemy's capabilities, and seek to supplant the insurgent's role. This does not mean they should be "irregular" in the sense of being brutal, or outside proper control. Rather, they should move, fight and organize like the insurgents – but have access to your support and be under the firm control of their parent societies, cemented by close ties to local social networks. Combined with a mobilized population and trusted networks, this allows local forces to "hard-wire" the enemy out of the environment, under the cover of security from you. At the company level, this means that raising, training and employing local indigenous auxiliary forces (police and military) are valid tasks. This requires high-level clearance, of course, but if such support is given, you should establish a training cell in your company. Platoons should aim to train one local squad, then use that squad as a nucleus for a partner platoon, and the company headquarters should train an indigenous leadership team. This mirrors the "growth" process of other trusted networks, and tends to emerge naturally as you win local allies – who naturally want to take up arms in their own defense.

23. **Practice armed civil affairs.** Counterinsurgency is armed social work: it is an attempt to redress basic social and political problems while being shot at. This makes civil affairs a central counterinsurgency activity, not an afterthought. It is how we restructure the environment to deny the enemy a role in it. In your company sector, civil affairs must focus on meeting basic needs first, then progress up Maslow's hierarchy as each successive need is met. You need intimate cooperation with inter-agency partners here – national, international and local. Our role is to provide protection, identify needs, facilitate civil affairs and use improvements in social conditions as leverage to build networks and mobilize the population. Thus, there is no such thing as impartial humanitarian assistance or civil affairs in counterinsurgency. Every action we take to help someone hurts someone else – not least the insurgents. So civil and humanitarian assistance personnel will be targeted. Protecting them is a matter not only of close-in defense, but also of creating a

permissive operating environment by co-opting the beneficiaries of aid – local communities and leaders – to help us help them.

24. **Small is beautiful.** Another natural tendency is to go for large-scale, mass programs. In particular, we have a tendency to template ideas that succeed in one area and transplant them into another, and we tend to take small programs that work and try to replicate them on a larger scale. Again, this is usually a mistake – often programs succeed because of specific local conditions of which we are unaware, or because their very smallness kept them below the enemy's radar and helped them flourish unmolested. At the company level, programs that succeed in one district often also succeed in another (because the overall company sector is small), but small-scale projects rarely proceed smoothly into large programs. Keep programs small: this makes them cheap, sustainable, low-key and (importantly) recoverable if they fail. You can add new programs – also small, cheap and tailored to local conditions – as the situation allows.

25. **Fight the enemy's strategy, not his forces.** At this stage, if things are proceeding well, your networks are displacing the enemy and your "single narrative" is bearing fruit, the insurgents will go over to the offensive. Yes, the *offensive* – because you have created an overall situation so dangerous to the insurgents, by threatening to displace them from the environment, that they have to attack you and the population in order to get back into the game. Thus it is normal, even in the most successful operations, to have sudden spikes of offensive insurgent activity late in the campaign. This does not necessarily mean you have done something wrong (though it may: it depends on whether you have successfully mobilized the population). At this point the tendency is to go for the jugular and seek to destroy the enemy's forces in open battle. This is almost never the best choice at company level, because provoking major combat usually plays into the enemy's hands by undermining the population's confidence. Instead, attack the enemy's strategy: if he is seeking to recapture the allegiance of a segment of the local population, then coopt them against him. If he is trying to provoke a sectarian conflict, go over to "peace enforcement mode" and work on convincing his co-religionists to sell him out in return for security. The permutations are endless but the principle is the same – fight the enemy's strategy, not his forces.

124

26. **Build your own solution – only attack the enemy when he gets in the way.** Again, as the campaign develops, the insurgents will be increasingly marginalized, violent and desperate. Opportunities will arise to target the enemy, perhaps killing large numbers. Try not to be distracted by this. Your aim should be to implement your own solution – the "game plan" you developed early in the campaign, and then refined through interaction with local partners. Your approach must be environment-centric (based on dominating the whole district and implementing a solution to its systemic problems) rather than enemy-centric. This means that, particularly late in the campaign, you may need to learn to negotiate with the enemy. Members of the population that supports you also know the enemy's leaders – they may have grown up together in the small district that is now your company area – and valid negotiating partners sometimes emerge as the campaign progresses. Again, you need close inter-agency relationships to exploit opportunities to coopt segments of the enemy. This helps you wind down the insurgency without alienating potential local allies who have relatives or friends in the insurgent movement. At this stage, a defection is better than a surrender, a surrender is better than a capture, and a capture is better than a kill.

Getting Short

Time is short, and the tour is drawing to a close. The key problem now is keeping your people focused, preventing them from dropping their guard and maintaining the rage on all the multifarious programs, projects and operations that you have started. In this final phase, the previous articles still stand, but there is an important new one:

27. **Keep your extraction plan secret.** The temptation to talk about home becomes almost unbearable toward the end of a tour. The locals know you are leaving, and probably have a better idea than you of the generic extraction plan – remember, they have seen units come and go. But you must protect the specific details of the extraction plan, or the enemy will use this as an opportunity to score a high-profile hit, re-capture the population's allegiance by scare tactics that convince them they will not be protected once you leave, or persuade them that your successor unit will be oppressive or incompetent. Keep the details secret, within a tightly controlled

compartment in your headquarters. And resist the temptation to say goodbye to local allies: you can always send a postcard from home.

Conclusion

This, then, is the tribal wisdom, the folklore which those who went before you have learned. Like any folklore it needs interpretation, and contains seemingly contradictory advice. Over time, as you study your sector, you will learn to apply these ideas, and will add to this store of wisdom from your own observations and experience. So only one article remains; and if you remember nothing else, remember this:

28. **Break any rule, sooner than lose the initiative.** In counterinsurgency, the initiative is everything. If the enemy is reacting to you, you control the operation and, provided you mobilize the population, you will win. If you are reacting to the enemy – even if you are killing or capturing him in large numbers – then he is controlling the environment and you will eventually lose. This is because, in counterinsurgency, the enemy almost always has the tactical initiative. He initiates most attacks, targets you unexpectedly and withdraws too fast for you to react. So instead, you must focus on the local population, build your own solution to the environment and its systemic problems, further your own game plan and fight the enemy only when he gets in the way. This helps you keep the initiative.

Dr. David Kilcullen served 21 years in the Australian Army. He commanded an infantry company on counterinsurgency operations in East Timor, taught counterinsurgency tactics as an exchange instructor at the British School of Infantry, served as a military advisor to Indonesian Special Forces and trained and led Timorese irregular troops. He has worked in several Middle East countries with regular and irregular police and military forces since 9/11, and was a special adviser for Irregular Warfare during the 2005 U.S. Quadrennial Defense Review. He is currently seconded to the U.S. State Department as Chief Strategist in the Office of the Coordinator for Counterterrorism, and remains a Reserve Lieutenant Colonel in the Australian Army. His doctoral dissertation is a study of Indonesian insurgent and terrorist groups and counterinsurgency methods.

Improvised Explosive Devices

Improvised Explosive Devices (IEDs) are the preferred insurgent weapon for several reasons; they're a low "personal risk weapon" for the insurgent, they're effective casualty causing tools, they're cheap to make, relatively easy to build, require little training to employ, and are easily exploited for propaganda purposes.

Although IEDs are at times used for tactical purposes, such as delaying a unit's movement or temporarily denying a unit access to an area, *their main purpose and effect is psychological and informational.* By creating a great deal of destruction and unpredictability, IEDs generate fear, and inevitably, overreaction by the counterinsurgency force, which eventually causes a lack of trust and confidence between the local populace and the force. IEDs also generate media attention which extends fear to the international community breaking down the will of the civilian populace within the coalition. The enemy's exploitation of IED attacks through an unwitting media is critical to undercutting the host nation. Small unit leaders must comprehend this and take it in stride in order to keep their subordinates undismayed by these events. There are 4 main types of IEDs: *time operated; command operated; victim operated;* and *projected weapons.*

Time Operated

Time operated IEDs give an insurgent the ability to vacate the area before detonation, allowing him to separate himself from the situation avoiding possible capture or harm. They are easy to build and can use timers that vary from sophisticated electronic timers such as cell phones to those as primitive as blocks of ice. There are four types of time operated IEDs[1]

- *"Igniferous"*—Slow burning items leading to a detonator, such as cigarettes. The device is simple to make and employ.

---

[1] U.K. Royal Army Land Warfare Center, *Stability Operations Handbook*, Mission Support Group 2006

127

- *Indicators:* Small traces of smoke or steam coming from a hidden or recessed area, such as an open trash can; Faint burning odor in otherwise "clean" air; Normally populated area is vacant; Items shifted to make space, such as small clearing in a trash pile.

- *Chemical*—Simple device, mixing two chemicals to create a reaction and detonate a larger charge. A good example of this is a condom or balloon containing sulphuric acid inserted into a chlorate/sugar main charge. Acid eats through the rubber and ignites the chlorate/sugar mix on contact. The time can be altered by adding additional layers of rubber.

  - *Indicators*: Vacancy of a usually populated area; Recently moved items; Odd placed or out of place packages, such as briefcases or boxes

- *Mechanical*—Most common form of timers. In their least sophisticated form a watch or alarm clock can be used; these are less reliable than electro-mechanical timers, which are made from appliance timers. These devices can be set for up to twelve hours but are more commonly set for less than one.

  - *Indicators*: Vacancy of a usually populated area: Faint or strong ticking sounds; Faint sound of mechanical movements (like the wind of a kitchen timer); Recently moved items; Odd placed or out of place packages

- *Electronic*—Provide longer and more accurate delays. Cellular phones, electronic timers, digital watches and video recorders are a few of the devices that can be used, or the timer can be made from scratch.

  - *Indicators:* Vacancy of a usually populated area; Recently moved items; Odd placed or out of place packages.

Command Operated

This type of device allows the insurgent to choose the moment for detonation. They are effective against moving targets such as convoys and patrols at choke points and along routes with set patterns. The sophistication of this type of device is constantly changing. As technologies are developed to defeat the detonators insurgents change the types and complexities of the device. EOD units will attempt to disarm these devices in order to render it ineffective meanwhile finding new insurgent technologies. There are two types of command operated IEDs:

- **Command Linked**—This type of device is physically linked from the firing point to the contact point. **Types of links:** Wire—using electronic pulse to detonate; Pull—using a pull wire to detonate; Explosive—using a series of explosions to detonate (similar to det cord); Fiber-Optic.

  - *Indicators:* Exposed wires; Recently moved debris; Recently dug holes; Moved pavement; Vacancy of usually populated areas; Odd placed packages or objects; Recently moved objects.

- **Command Separated**—This type of device has no physical link to the explosive. It is easier to conceal and is limited to the range of the trigger. There are a wide range of triggers from cell phones to garage door openers that can be used; all that is required is a transmitter and receiver. **Types of unlinked triggers:** Radio Control; Light Command; Active Infra Red; Projectile Command.

  - *Indicators:* Recently moved debris; Recently dug holes; Moved pavement; Vacancy of usually populated areas; Odd placed packages or objects; Recently moved objects.

Victim Operated

A Victim Operated IED, often referred to as a "booby trap", uses a set trigger that is tripped by the intended target. They are useful in creating entry deterrence and restricting or slowing the movement of a unit. Most IEDs generate psychological effect, causing units to move cautiously through areas and denying them cover. Common methods are:

- **Pull/Trip**—Victim physically changes the balance of the device by tripping a hidden line or cord

- **Pressure**—Functions by applying weight or pressure to the switch, can use either a micro-switch or pressure mat.

- *Pressure Release*—Usually using micro-switches, when the depressed switch is released and resets itself the device is triggered. This works well with opening objects such as the lid of a storage box or foot locker.

- *Movement Sensitive*—Uses reed, trembler or mercury tilt switches and will detonate upon disturbance.

- *Light Sensitive*—Uses light, either natural or artificial, to trigger a reaction. Light meters that move to a contact piece and Light Sensitive Diodes (LSDs) that allow current to flow with increased light are two examples of Light Sensitive IEDs.

- *Electronic*—Examples are: Relays and Silicon Controlled Rectifiers (SCRs) used as collapsing circuits, which cause the IED to detonate when wires are cut or start secondary timers after an initial explosion or EOD response. Devices sensitive to radio signals also work off of electronic triggers. Passive Infra Red and Active Infra Red systems use a "break beam" or "make beam" system respectively, much like the safety beam on an automatic garage door.

  – *Indicators:* Recently moved debris; Recently dug holes; Vacancy of usually populated areas; Odd placed packages or objects; Recently moved objects; Wires or missed placed electronic devices.

Projected Weapons

This type of IED normally uses either existing operational ordnance such as a mortar round or fabricated ordnance such as a handcrafted grenade. The system of delivery is limited by the insurgent's imagination. Types of Projected Weapons follow: Indirect fire mortars; Direct fire mortars; Rockets and rocket propelled grenades; Projected, dropped and thrown grenades; Guided weapons. There are several methods by which insurgents can deliver IEDs that include:

- *Vehicle Borne IED (VBIED)*—VBIEDs can be used to either time detonate, victim detonate or command detonate from a static position. They can also be used either as a moving device delivering explosives to a static position such as a vehicle check point, or to destroy moving targets, such as the lead vehicle in a convoy. In any case, they can hold a great deal of explosives and create extensive damage.

- *Roadside IEDs*—Normally used to disrupt/destroy convoys and patrols along commonly used routes and choke points. They are often accompanied with direct and indirect fire ambushes.

- *Trash can bombs and packages*—Normally time or command detonated however, they can be victim detonated by lifting a lid or opening a package or briefcase. These types of IEDs are used as anti-personnel devices targeting search teams and patrols.

- *Suicide Bombers*—Wearing vests, belts, or carrying packages, suicide bombers truly enhance the psychological effect of an IED. Once this element occurs in theater every person becomes suspect. They are difficult to detect and even more difficult to defeat. Often the bomber is a willing fanatic; however, in some desperate cases the bomber's family is being held ransom or is in some type of desperate situation, making the action even more unpredictable. Often times, signs of a suicide bomber include a great deal of sweating due to the weight of the explosive, unseasonably heavy clothes, odd behavior (nervousness) or a distinct chemical odor.

- *Trip Wires and Booby Traps*—Often used as anti-personnel devices to delay or temporarily deny access to an area. They are also used to disrupt patrols and "wear down" units psychologically. They can range from simple trip wires on doors and walls to advanced switches.

131

CPSIA information can be obtained
at www.ICGtesting.com
Printed in the USA
BVHW040203310122
627606BV00011B/351

9 781780 390291